What Is
Your Life's Work?

also by Bill Jensen

Simplicity
The New Competitive Advantage in a World of More, Better, Faster

Work 2.0
Building the Future, One Employee at a Time

The Simplicity Survival Handbook
32 Ways to Do Less and Accomplish More

for more: www.ourlifeswork.com • www.simplerwork.com

For information, address HarperCollins Publishers, Inc.,
10 East 53rd Street, New York, NY 10022.

HarperCollins books may be purchased for educational,
business, or sales promotional use.
For information please write:
Special Markets Department,
HarperCollins Publishers, Inc.,
10 East 53rd Street, New York, NY 10022.

FIRST EDITION

Designed by Bill Jensen.
Production by Aimee Leary, Final Art Design Group.

Library of Congress Cataloging-in-Publication Data
Jensen, Bill
    What is your life's work: answer the big question about what really
matters—and reawaken the passion for what you do. Bill Jensen
        p. cm.
    "With inspiring stories from people who found their way."
    Includes index.
    ISBN 0-06-076686-7
    1. Self-realization. 2. Interpersonal relations. 3. Job satisfaction.
    4. Happiness. I. Title.

    BJ1470.J46 2005
    158.6—dc22
                        2005040275

05 06 07 08 09 RRD 10 9 8 7 6 5 4 3 2 1

What Is
Your Life's Work?

Answer the big question about

what really matters...

and reawaken the passion for what you do.

HarperBusiness

An Imprint of HarperCollins*Publishers*

What Is Your Life's Work?

Answer the big question about what really matters…
and reawaken the passion for what you do.

Contents

What Is Your Life's Work?

An Owner's Manual

You are holding our collective life's work:
that is, how we continually figure out what matters,
and what doesn't.

What Is Your Life's Work? captures the intimate
exchanges between mothers and daughters, fathers
and sons, and caring teammates and friends — all
talking about what matters at work, and in life. Its
pages are filled with the personal letters and journal
entries of well-known leaders, struggling managers,
and heroic people in workaday jobs.

It is a practical guide for work-weary souls trying to
get unstuck, as well as those who already do a lot of
what matters, and just want to do more. Exposed are
the raw truths we've all experienced, the personal
frailties and mistakes we'd like to hide, and the
proudest achievements we'd like to celebrate.

How to Use This Book
Find the few that speak to you.

1. Do not read cover-to-cover. Find three to five letters that speak directly to you. Not every one will. That's OK.

Your job: Find the letters that grab you, inspire you, teach you, and challenge you. (To search letters by themes, see page 223.)

2. The book is divided into five discoveries you'll experience in your life's work. Which discovery contained two or more of the letters you selected in Step 1? That's the theme for writing your own letter…

3. Write a letter to a loved one.

Take something from this book and pay it forward.

You'll get back even more than you give.

(Field Guide for Getting Started is on page 209.)

Continue Your Journey
Visit www.ourlifeswork.com

- Personal stories from diarists, unpublished letters, plus full versions of those letters edited for space

- Workshops and presentations available for your group

- Additional how-to tools and support for letter-writing

- Community space for sharing stories and experiences

- Bonus: Get YOUR letter into the paperback version! We are taking submissions for additional letters. We will select the most powerful letter(s) for inclusion in the paperback version of *What Is Your Life's Work?* Cool, huh?!

Your Life's Work

...

You are about to experience something extraordinary...

• • •

Imagine having a profound, plain-spoken conversation with your loved ones.

You share how you figured out what matters and what doesn't. You speak with absolute conviction: "This is what I stood for, believed in, struggled with, and accomplished. This is my life's work, and what I want to be remembered for."

Never before have you experienced such clarity. Suddenly, everything makes sense. Wow! Where did all this clarity of purpose come from? The answer lies in the magical journey within this book.

"Never in my life have I been so clear about what really matters...." Everyone who shared their biggest lessons-learned discovered something for themselves — profound clarity, and reawakened passion for what they do. You can find that, too!

That's because this book does not shy away from difficult introspection. Every page deals with one powerful question: What would you tell your kids or grandkids or dearest friends about what really matters at work? If they asked:

- How do I know I'm making a difference?
- What's the real reason I'm here?
- Is this all there is?
- How much is too much?
- How do I decide: Stay or go?

How would you answer? Would you tell the whole truth — including all the naive mistakes you've made — to help them figure out what did and didn't matter?

What Is Your Life's Work? reveals it all: The poor choices we've made and the lessons we've learned from those choices, as well as our proudest moments.

Put simply, this book is about what we learn about ourselves when we teach our loved ones, especially our kids, what matters, and about the powerful need we have to leave something behind — what we want to be remembered for.

The Surprising Discovery Behind This Book

I've spent my career listening to people just like you and me — collecting our stories, and studying how we work. During the past two decades, I've interviewed and surveyed more than 400,000 people in over 1,000 companies around the world. My first question — "What really matters here?" — never failed to jumpstart insightful conversations. That is, until a few years ago.

After the economy took a painful nosedive, lots of people backed away from that question. They did not want to admit that what mattered to their company — the bottom line and corporate survival above all else — was suddenly quite different from what mattered to them. And that they were slogging through every day just to keep their job.

So I tried changing the question. I asked instead, "What is the single most important insight about work that you want to pass on to your kids? Or to anyone you truly care about?"

BAM! The floodgates opened.

A happy accident: Changing my question to something much closer to home, "Why do we do what we wouldn't want our kids to do? Which of our mistakes should they not repeat?" unleashed completely new conversations.

After just a few interviews, I asked people to put their thoughts on paper: "Write a letter to that loved one. Or keep a journal — a work diary. One that would help your kids or someone else who is close to you understand what's truly important at work."

The invitation to write something for a loved one spread through word of mouth and email. Soon, what began as a small experiment grew into a global collection of several thousand letters, gathered over a four-year period. You are holding a representative sampling from that collection.

Why were so many so willing to spend time on these letters? Because as they were writing to change their children's future or to help others, something magical happened. They got back more than they gave.

That's what makes this approach to discovering what really matters so different from anything you've experienced. You end up getting what you want — deeper clarity around what's most important to you — by giving it to someone else. Your work diary for others ends up being a tool for self-discovery.

That's how an administrative assistant discovered that she was actually a leader — by writing to her unborn daughter. And how the son of a tuna fisherman and how a former go-go dancer uncovered the power of saying yes to their dreams. And how a lawyer rediscovered rights and wrongs.

In their letters, we see ourselves.

From a student we learn about hard work and

passion. From a teacher about distinguishing between your own goals and those imposed upon you. From a prison guard we learn about caring, forgiveness, and limitless possibilities. We learn about shattered trust from the entire family of an executive who was fired over politics. About the power of asking questions and listening to "poor performers" from a former monk, now an executive. About the cost of over-investing in an employer from a former corporate lifer.

In their struggles, we see our own.

Our Struggle to Figure Out What Really Matters

Most of us experience a disconnect between what we're supposed to get done at work and what truly matters.

According to over 40 Gallup studies, about 75% of us are disengaged from our jobs. That shows up in our pursuit of what really matters: According to the most recent U.S. Job Retention Survey, 75% of all employees are now searching for new employment opportunities. We're voting with our feet! And the New American Dream Survey found that more than four out of every five of us (83%) wish we had more of what really matters in life.

Traumatic touchstones such as 9/11 and the tsunami in Asia have connected us all in a collective search for what truly matters. This search is no longer a nice-to-do. It's real. It's urgent.

And then there's work complexity. My own research shows that the biggest reasons we work so hard have a lot less to do with the economy, or market forces, or the competition, than we are led to believe. Much of our work, as well as the processes and tools we're handed, are unnecessarily complicated, unfocused, poorly designed, and confusing! Result: Most of us are sleeping less, stressed out more, trying to cram too many to-do's into every day, and are still left wondering which of our actions really mattered.

In my travels, I not only compile statistics like these, I also feel everyone's utter exhaustion. Whether it's in Atlanta or Albuquerque, Stockholm or Singapore — I see the stress on everyone's faces, and hear it in their pleas for change. And what's our payback for working this hard, this much? Almost two-thirds of us haven't received a meaningful "Attaboy!" in the past year. Half of us are very concerned about job security — twice as many as five years ago. Companies are even sending sheriffs to deliver court summonses to retirees — we're now suing past employees so we don't have to pay their promised pensions! Geez…Where are we heading?

Work is not just an eight-hour interruption in our day. Most of us will spend most of our adult lives and most of our waking hours focused on our jobs. Whether we like it or not, we are defined by the choices we make at work. How we behave during that time is often the most documented record of who we are, what we stand for, and what we believe. One senior vice president at a Fortune 50 company has resorted to bringing home pictures of her co-workers so she can explain to her four-year-old why Mommy spends so much time away from him. Is this the record we want to leave for our kids — a photo album of team meetings?

There's an irony in all the warm and fuzzy

business talk of the past decade. Despite a heightened emphasis on people issues, our work contract still carries this built-in conflict: Individuals are constantly asked to sacrifice their own needs for the good of the company (or customer or boss). And most of us really struggle with this conflict.

Which means that the need to look deep inside ourselves has never been more critical, more urgent.

What won't change is the pressure; the drive for ever-higher productivity will not go away. Everyone is being asked to do more with less. And most of the *more* is not what we really want to do.

What's got to change is the choices we make. And the personal values we choose to follow instead of the constant pressure to produce *morebetterfaster*. With every choice we make at work, we take a stand for what we believe. Or not. We practice what we preach. Or not. We focus on what really matters to us. Or not. We adhere to the same guiding principles that we follow when we're outside of work. Or not.

We need to be more aware of the hundreds of tiny choices we make every day that lead us away from, or toward, what really matters. We need the guts to understand and learn from those choices. To find the steel and the compass that reside in us all.

My Life's Work:
Personal Discoveries Behind This Book

Over ten years ago, a wake-up call completely changed my life's work, and pulled me into this project.

In July 1994, I came home one night just as the phone was ringing. It was my sister. Mom just had a massive stroke. We'd better get to the hospital — fast.

We got there just in time for the emergency room doctor to inform us that Mom wasn't expected to make it through the night. None of us was prepared for this shock. Mom was the cornerstone of our family. Suddenly, we had to say goodbye.

Since there was nothing more that could be done, we were told she would be moved from Emergency to the Intensive Care Unit on another floor. We were asked to go to the ICU waiting room, and assured that we could rejoin her in just a few minutes. Five minutes went by: No Mom. Ten minutes. Twenty, thirty, almost forty minutes passed — no Mom. Finally, I went ballistic. I stormed into the nurses' station, screaming, cursing, demanding to know where she was.

What happened? Poor communication between the two departments. Nobody in the ICU knew that Audrey Jensen was supposed to be moved there. The doctors apologized profusely, and got us to her bedside as quickly as possible. A few hours later, Mom passed away.

For months, I scribbled down what I was going through and thinking about. Eventually, a new kind of clarity emerged for me. I found a new calling — what really mattered in my own work became crystal clear.

Those notes thrust me into a discovery that no one else was talking about. I realized that everything a company does uses a portion of its people's lives, and it is a leader's responsibility to make sure that their time is used wisely. Because once time is gone, it's gone forever. There are only 1440 minutes in every day. No do-overs. Time stolen from you at work means less time for whatever really matters to you.

You see, most business people would unpack my experience in that hospital from a communications perspective, or cost or process-failure perspective, or customer (patient) care perspective. Yes, all those views are right...but they're not what really matters!

Even though it wasn't intentional, when that hospital screwed up, they stole from me 40 of the last minutes I would ever have with Mom. I will never get those minutes back.

I now apply what I discovered — that we must all be respectful of how work uses the precious time in people's lives — as a guiding principle in whatever I do every day. I've fired clients because a dozen senior execs weren't willing to talk to each other for a few hours (creating alignment among the leadership team), but were willing to ask employees to use millions of person-hours to accomplish company goals without that alignment. I've cut communication programs from hundreds of pages down to one. I've upset some executives because my research found their "best" practices to be too complicated and disrespectful.

I can draw a direct line between what happened in the hospital that night, my diary about the experience, and how that changed what really mattered for me. I used to just help managers and execs lead more effectively; now I also battle for business's soul. I'm a passionate defender against anything that wastes your time at work, so you can take more control of your life.

However, your moment of clarity doesn't have to come from some life-altering, traumatic experience. It can be drawn out by something as painless as writing a letter to a loved one. I've found that people just like you have created the space they needed to uncover their calling and truly hear their own voice simply by writing down the choices they've made, and how those choices got them where they are today. As I pored over thousands of letters, a pattern emerged: There were not one or two, but five moments of deep clarity in everyone's search for what really matters. Five basic discoveries we all can experience.

• • •

The 5 Moments of Clarity Discoveries on Your Journey

No matter where you go, there you are: at the point of discovery. I've found teenagers who have encountered the "final" discovery of finding joy, serenity, and fulfillment, and retirees who are just now making time for the "first" one — finding themselves. These discoveries are not bound by career moves or age or life experience. They reveal themselves to you whenever you are open to them. What I can say is that the people who felt they were consistently focused on what really mattered had experienced three or more of these discoveries, and could clearly articulate the *how*, *when*, and *why* of each of those experiences.

Discovery *1*: Finding Yourself

Most everyone *already knows* what really matters, at work and everywhere else. We just let all the daily excuses and conflicting priorities cloud our judgment. Yet the people who are truly focused on what matters to them rarely have this problem. They know how to listen to themselves — how to quiet all the outside noise long enough to hear their own heartbeat and their own wisdom. Use the letters in this section to jumpstart deeper thinking about who you are and what matters to you.

Discovery *2*: Finding the Lessons to Be Learned, the Questions to Be Asked

You have a lifetime of hard-won wisdom, and you've spent years figuring out what to ask when tough choices are thrown at you. But it's easy to forget all that when confronted with the daily pressures in today's *morebetterfaster* workloads. Use this section to help you remember all the lessons you've learned, and pass that on to others.

Discovery *3*: Finding the Choices That Really Matter

Every day you face hundreds of tiny choices — which things to do, which people to see, what meetings to attend, what to say, how quickly to respond — all of which seem terribly urgent and pressing. But only a precious few choices will lead you to what really matters. Use the letters in this section to consider which choices in your day really do matter. Start a list: on one side, *Urgent and Pressured*; on the other, *Important to Me*. Compare how often you choose one side over the other. Is it time to choose differently?

Discovery *4*: Finding the Courage to Choose

Saying "no" to your boss, or just telling her something else she doesn't want to hear; taking on a project that's beyond your current skills; walking away from overtime when there are bills to be paid; finding a better job; or just ignoring that deluge of emails, all require some kind of courage. Most of these letter-writers discovered that once they found their inner clarity, courageous choices that had seemed hard became easy. Use this section to think about how that kind of clarity would make difficult choices a lot easier.

Discovery *5*: Finding Joy, Serenity, and Fulfillment

It's time to find the grace in most every challenge you face, most every choice you make, most every person you encounter. You can do it. There is a higher level of what really matters. Everyone who finds it will experience a transformational leap of knowing themselves and how they are connected to something bigger than themselves. The letters in this section provide a jumping-off point for you to know what that might look like for you. Keep in mind that this final discovery is different for each of us. One letter-writer described it as the joy of toil and hard work, another as the fulfillment of giving to others, and another as focusing on family above all else. What is your statement of grace? Who do you want to be?

Finding Your Voice:
A Field Guide for Getting Started

Somewhere on these pages are three to five letters

that speak so directly to you, it's as if they were authored by you. Their story is your story. Once you find those letters, it's time to jump to the Field Guide.

Pay it forward. Take something from this book — an inspirational story, a new way of thinking, a big Aha! about mistakes you've made, or one of the discoveries that meant the most to you — and write a letter to your loved ones.

The last section in this book is a guide for sharing what matters to you. It includes the gifts you can give to yourself and to others, as well as exercises designed to take you step-by-step through your own discoveries, and how to share them with your loved ones.

Believe me, you'll get back even more than you give.

Jump into an Extraordinary Experience

You are holding our collective life's work: that is, how we continually figure out what matters, and what doesn't.

By sharing what usually stays private, the letter-writers have opened a space that never existed before — a new way to see and know ourselves. Exposed are the raw truths we've all experienced. The personal frailties and mistakes we'd like to hide. And the proudest achievements we'd like to celebrate.

In their letters, you will find yourself.

Jump in!

Bill Jensen
bill@ourlifeswork.com

DISCOVERY

FINDING YOURSELF

"I want to reach inside myself through the muck and mire and live more with love and less with fear. I'm tired of waiting for that right person or company to recognize the talent that I can offer."

•••

"I'm a workaholic. I can't remember a time when I wasn't striving for full-throttle success. As it turns out, I failed in one critical area. I had turned my back on life."

•••

"The opposite of play is not work — it's psychosis."

We've all been there. We've felt feelings like these letter-writers have, and thought the same thoughts.

• • •

Most of us *already know* what
really matters.
We just let all the daily excuses and
conflicting priorities cloud our judgment.
I find this most everywhere I go
as I research how we get stuff done.
Yet the people who are truly focused
on what matters rarely have this problem.
They know how to listen to themselves —
how to quiet all the outside noise
long enough to hear their own heartbeat
and their own wisdom.

• • •

No one gives you inner knowing,
but here's a chance to discover it.

• • •

Hear what you think as you read
these letters. Allow each one to speak
for a portion of your own life.
Risk seeing yourself.

• • •

Face what you fear; it's safe here.
Get grounded; others are like you.
Let go; nobody's watching.
Suspend judgment;
other people's Aha's can reveal a lot.
Find your passion; write it down.
Laugh at your own excuses; a sense of humor
will make Discoveries 2–5 a lot easier!
Rewrite the script, because you can.

Let No One Tell You It Can't Be Done

Lisa Hesmondhalgh

Work: Helps and believes in society's rejects, where most of us would not

Lisa Hesmondhalgh has survived several lifetimes of renovating human psyches. As a police officer in Dade County, Florida, she learned the importance of performing CPR on a corpse. During her years as a prison guard, before she turned social worker, she discovered that shooting to stop and shooting to kill have more to do with luck than skill.

TO ALL MY CHILDREN,

Before I was 25, my sons and daughters were rapists, car jackers, burglars and robbers. I watched the true birth of my favorite child — on the day he turned 50 — from behind peeling beige paint and pockmarked prison bars. He stood in the hallway with a cardboard box ringed with twine. I opened the heavy metal door and stepped in to meet him.

"I want you to take care of yourself and the life you have left," I said. "There's nothing you're leaving here that matters at all."

I put my hand out and he shook it gently. He picked up the box, turned to walk outside, and said, "And you. Promise me you'll leave before they change you, before they get you, too."

Keith was being paroled after 28 years in prison, after 12 years on Death Row for murdering a store clerk with a shotgun. He had earned his G.E.D. and an Associate's degree. He became a journeyman plumber. He would eventually marry, keep a good blue-collar job, go to church twice each week, and probably never think of me again.

Before I was 30, my sons and daughters were crack addicts, embezzlers, child molesters, thieves and forgers. I went to their houses every week to make certain they were behaving. I went to see their teachers, their bosses, their lovers. They would telephone me after midnight when their uncles beat them with baseball bats and in the morning when they needed a ride to English-as-a-Second-Language class. They would come to see me when their last pair of shoes melted at their day-labor roofing job.

And when I was 35, my sons and daughters changed again. They were crumbled and torn and splintered and lost. My children were burned, raped, rented to ex-boyfriends for the weekend, and fed on cockroach cereal with bloodied heroin spoons.

I would find my children new homes with new families. And learn that their new families were forcing my daughters to give nude massages and were paying my sons to have sex with neighbors. I would find other homes, and my children had nightmares that were too loud, daymares with explosive hoofbeats — tempests of memories. My children had tears louder than their screams.

This letter is to those I have lived my life for. The convicted felons, the probationers and parolees, the ones who were called "clients" by my peers and treated like sewage.

Every introduction speech from me began: "I will not call you a client. You are a criminal. But

I promise that I will treat you as a person, as an individual. From now on, you will not fail unless you want to."

Offenders are the people you see in the next grocery aisle. They stand in the church pew behind you. And for ten years I was proud that I was never threatened, cursed, or assaulted by anyone on my caseload.

But jumping from Florida's criminal justice system to Child Protective Services in California was not a great career move. It was my personal San Andreas Fault.

I left social work to the better socialized. I was not tough enough, careless enough, or thoughtless enough to survive what my children were living through.

I retired to a small military base with my husband and one biological child. A child whose only nightmares include a domineering third-grade teacher and an occasional tarantula.

These are nightmares I can soothe with a hug. I can brush them away with explanations. The teacher is an oversized toothache. And the tarantula's name is Quentin. He makes films. And my child's laughter is my cue for survival.

To my other children — the ones behind bars — I bequeath my spirit of unrest. I send you a nagging, gnawing ability to harass anyone who tells you it can't be done, that you will never succeed, and that you cannot pull free from your past.

Now and forever, I gather each of you to a wake in honor of our collective failures. Let's bury them and dance on the graves of past Self-fulfilling Prophecies! Let's walk out and away from our bruised past. To a new future.

Lisa Hesmondhalgh recently moved from her last gig — living quietly with her family on a barren plantation in Guantánamo Bay, Cuba — teaching Ethics and Art Appreciation to heavily armed individuals. She now enjoys the Byronic weather patterns of the Pacific Northwest. Her current project is a true fictional account of her six years in Gitmo. And avoiding generic men with dark suits and Raybans in oversized SUVs with government license plates.

●●●

After Love, It's All About Trust

John Harvey

Work: Fishmonger, transitions coach, trusted friend

John Harvey's most recent position in corporate America was Senior Vice President of Global Talent at American Express. He left under difficult circumstances. He now pays the bills by selling fish. He's writing to his four kids.

DEAR JOHN, CORINNE, JANEAN, AND JULIA,

I have a new urgency in devoting my time to the most important things in life. This is why I made one of the most difficult decisions of my professional life — to leave American Express. Once I realized that I worked with some people who did not value what I had to offer, and whom I could not trust, I knew I couldn't waste another day there.

The one most significant lesson I could pass on to you is about trust. Specifically, "Be someone who can be trusted and know who you can trust."

I have learned that it starts with me, not with other people.

Being trusted means that I am willing and able to take responsibility for my actions and behavior — all the time. Being trusted means that I have earned honor and dignity because people have confidence that I will do the right thing. Trust means that my commitment to strong relationships with other people is grounded in honest, direct communication — telling the deepest truths. Trust means that I am true to my word and my values. Being trusted means that I honor my commitments, I am personally accountable, and I am willing to forgive.

I learned all these lessons because, during my last few years at American Express, I had the misfortune of working for someone who could not be trusted. It made my work very difficult, ineffective, and sad.

However, when you find people who you can trust — and they trust you — it is a wonderful feeling. Next to love, it's the best feeling in the world. Trust becomes the foundation for the relationships that will become the most important in your life.

After much soul-searching about what to do with the rest of his life, **John Harvey** recently became the proud owner of Freeman's Fish Market, in his hometown of Maplewood, New Jersey. But the process of his being fired and needing to figure out what to do so affected his family that they, too, decided to contribute letters. On the following pages are letters from John's wife, Helen, and three of his four children, Janean, Corinne, and John Jr. (Julia was a bit young for letter-writing) — all written while John was still in the throes of figuring out what to do after being fired.

Figuring It Out Together

Helen Harvey

Work: Helps a family focus on what's important

DEAR KIDS,

As long as I can remember I knew that I wanted to be a mother. A mother very different from my own, as she worked full-time outside of the house and I hated it. Growing up, I felt kind of cheated — that my relationship with her wasn't "enough" for her. Because of this, I made a commitment to myself very early on that I would be a stay-at-home mom.

Not so easy. When the first of you were born, my boss thought that being just a mom wouldn't be "enough" for me, and that she would help me continue to work. She offered me full-time pay for a part-time job. I took the bait and continued to work the equivalent of two full-time jobs for (three children and) five years.

During those years, I often sat outside by myself, watching the households that were run by nannies. I wondered if the kids in those homes felt like I did way back when — that they really didn't need that big a house, or all the stuff, and would have preferred to have their moms at home. Since you were too young to tell me, I wondered how you felt.

Finally, I came to the realization that by stretching myself so thin I was compromising what I really wanted — to have a great relationship with you, and to be the mom that I knew I could be.

Being a stay-at-home mom was wonderful while it lasted. Now, everything has changed.

For years, Dad was a great Company Man. Then suddenly, without warning, his years of stellar performance, A+ ratings, and continued promotions just weren't "enough." Even everything he did on 9/11 — making sure he was the last to leave the floor, and helping others out of his building before the neighboring Twin Towers collapsed — didn't matter. Shortly after, he reluctantly left American Express.

So we have been put to the task of pulling together as a family to help Dad find another job, while asking ourselves what is important and how much of what we already have do we really need.

I will admit to being hurt and angry about this. While Dad is out of work, and many others have been let go due to the economy, some executives who stayed are worrying over whether their bonus should be 12 million dollars instead of 10 million! They let people go to make their own performance look better, even though the very people who made them successful are now hurting.

Dad and I, however, haven't been much better. We prospered and accumulated to the point of owning a second home on the shore, while we knew there were people out there who could barely afford to eat. Dad worked harder and longer hours, and we spent less time with the people we love just to continue to build a "better" life. 9/11 was a giant message for all of us to start getting it right.

As we walk with Dad down this path of finding new work, we need your help.

How much is enough? What do you feel you need to have a happy life? What do we need to do to have the best relationship that we can with each other? How can we be more aware and take responsibility for the needs of others? How can we teach you resourcefulness?

Write us a letter. Tell us what you think is so important that you can't live without it.

Even better: Let's use all our letters to create a lifelong conversation. About what makes you happy, and what you think about our work. And about what will make you happy when you go to work.

Love, Mom

Helen Harvey describes herself as a mom and a wannabe several other things. Ask John about that, and he'll tell you she has been the foundation upon which his personal transition was built.

• • •

Mom, Dad: We Trust You to Do the Right Thing

Janean Harvey

12 years old
She chose the Q&A format, and wrote both the questions and answers

DEAR MOM AND DAD,

Q: What is it that we really need to have a good life?
A: I think that it's having a family that loves you,

friends that are actually your friends, a roof over your head, necessities, and maybe a few luxuries.

Q: How can you make our lives the best for us?
A: Just love us, listen to what we have to say, and provide us with food, drink, and clothes.

Q: If we needed the money, do we think Mom should go back to work?
A: No, because I like it that you're home all the time.

Q: What type of job do we think Dad should look for?
A: Something nearby, so we don't have to move.

Q: Is all that we have now really important?
A: No. We don't need a computer, or a TV, or a second house. Those things are luxuries, not necessities.

Corinne Harvey
15 years old

DEAR MOM AND DAD,

You have both given so much to us already. So first, I'd like to say thank you. Whether it was going to work each day to make our lives better and/or staying at home with us, you both have helped us to grow into better and happier people.

Both of you have brought a ton of happiness into my life. I think that all I really need to be happy is my family. I need someone there to help me see "the light at the end of the tunnel." Mom, you help me see this best. You are the ultimate optimist.

Having you as a stay-at-home mom is very important to me. If you really have to go back to work, I will understand. But I think that something would definitely be lacking without you around as much as you are. Many of my friends' moms work, and I think that they lack that special — yet strange — relationship you and I have. You are my best friend, and if you weren't home I just don't think things would really be the same.

Dad, you and I had a conversation about how I seem standoffish from you and have a "too cool" attitude. I just want to say I'm sorry. I love you, and even if sometimes I act too cool for you, inside I don't think I'll ever be. I made a comment to Mom about wanting you to get a "real job." I felt kinda bad after saying that. I think that financial stability seems pretty important to me. We have so much — maybe too much — and I think I take that for granted. I get a little materialistic sometimes, and fail to realize that in the long run, all of our wants aren't so important. Because of your and Mom's hard work, there aren't many times when one of us can say that we honestly "need" something.

I think we can give up a lot. There are many things that mean close to nothing, and that I'll probably be better off without.

We have been blessed with great lives, and I know that I would be lucky to have half as good a life when I grow up. I've also been blessed with parents as good as both of you and I think that even people out of our family realize that love you have for everyone. Because of your hard work we have been able to enjoy a life that many people only dream of.

So again, thank you. I love you both with my whole heart.

Love, Corrine

John Harvey, Jr.
17 years old

DEAR MOM AND DAD,

Up until a few months ago, my mindset was "Just keep bringing in the dough, Dad."

I didn't realize all the consequences of the long, hard hours you were working. Like missing out on some things in our lives as we were growing up. And maybe not being able to pursue things that you really wanted to do because you were working for us.

All my life I have striven to avoid work. I've had a few jobs but, to me, having a job is a burden.

Now that neither of you is working, I say "Congratulations!" You are free.

Sure, I realize that there is a need for some kind of income. But, if you have to work, do something that you want to do, not something that you think you have to do. That's the advice that you guys have always given me. And if you don't want to work, don't work.

Just do what you want to do, as long as it makes you happy.

Love, John

Harvey Diaries Postscript:

Trust is still a big issue. Even in a small business, like a fish store in a suburban bedroom community. After a few months of nurturing his employees — getting to know each one, placing personal notes of encouragement and goal-setting in every paycheck envelope, struggling to find affordable healthcare, working side-by-side with them in every job — John discovered mounting losses. A couple of employees were found lying and stealing, which affected the company and John's family significantly. Even though he took immediate action, John is still deeply hurt. Those individuals violated his trust. However, John Harvey still firmly believes in the inherent goodness of people. He volunteers a lot of his time to help others through their own career transitions. As a family, the Harveys chose to move into a smaller house, reducing monthly expenses so Helen could remain a stay-at-home mom.

···

Look Inside, Then Let Go

Jacquelyn Rardin

Work: Helps companies better communicate with the world

Jacquelyn Rardin is a learning-as-she-goes mother, an often dramatic, challenging and oddly loving wife, a respected public relations professional, and a part-time freelance writer and painter. She is writing to her daughter, Zoë.

DEAR ZOË,

I suspect, since you have some of my DNA, you very well may be predisposed to some of my personality traits or tendencies. So I hope these insights will help you someday when you are confronted with making choices in the workplace based on life direction.

First of all: I'm a workaholic.

I can't remember a time when I wasn't striving for full-throttle success. Aside from some innate ability, my drive was most likely fueled by my desire for attention, among other things. When I did well, my parents responded positively to me. I was worthy when I otherwise was nonexistent.

From toddlerhood, I've always had this desire to overachieve, to do better than everyone else. Even to outdo my best bests. By the time I was eight, I was already a published newspaper writer. By fifteen, I was off to college. You get the picture.

After college, in my first "real" job, I thought that achieving success was learning as much as possible, taking on as much responsibility as I could (and wanted!) and exceeding all expectations, delivering quality results without compromising my work ethics and career goals. This, of course, brought me respect, promotions, higher salaries, and a comfortable lifestyle.

I was fairly successful ten years later when I finally, and completely, burnt out.

As it turns out, I failed in one critical area in achieving true success. I had turned my back on life.

My life was void of actual living. While friends were off enriching their lives by taking days off, going out of town, taking in an exhibit, eating at the newest hip restaurant or volunteering time at the local animal shelter, I was filling up on more projects.

My life was work. And work was life.

I didn't even know how to enjoy life without the pleasures of meeting deadlines ahead of schedule or the tickling joy of working throughout the night. Pretty weird, eh?

At that time, I had moved across state lines three times (and out of the country on a part-time basis!), moved through countless corporate reorganizations and adapted an insomniac lifestyle, as working around the clock will do. I managed to accumulate extra weight faster than I could say the word *weight* — and, oh yeah, did I mention that I met your father at work, somehow fitting a relationship into this manic landscape of mine?

I had to stop and actually remember who I was. And you know what? I had no clue. For the first time in my life, I was dumbfounded. Lost. Overwhelmed. Scared.

Taking a deep breath and mustering up every reserve possible, I stepped off the endless treadmill I had created.

I let go.

Floating in a very uncomfortable space, I began an introspective journey in the hope of finding myself and what truly mattered. During this process, I came up with the following:

1. **I matter.** I deserve to have time to myself and to eat healthy and be an active participant in the world around me.

2. **My husband matters.** I had been seeing less and less of him and I missed our relationship.

3. **Doing the work I love matters.** There had to be a way for me to get paid for doing something that I am passionate about without consuming me whole.

4. **A place to call home matters.** While moving around so much, buying a house never made any sense and apartment living never gave me a good feeling of "being home."

5. Meeting new people and exploring local cultural opportunities matters. What do people do outside of the office? I'm going to find out!

With this new perspective, I embraced life with the same delicious fervor I had applied to my career.

Little by little, I started eating better and being more honest with myself (and others) on when I needed a break. I became reacquainted with your father, giggling in delight as we talked throughout the night about non-work-related ideas and dreams. I began to work with nonprofits in developing arts education programs, while also taking some time off to simply explore, taste and see the world around me.

For a while, life and work couldn't have been better. That's when you came along and I realized life could be AMAZING!

I saw becoming a mother as one of my biggest, most frightening and rewarding roles of my life. But for me, it was like, "Why quit work? I love what I do! I just need to make room for my new role." And it didn't take long before I was back on the same treadmill...running double time.

That is, until reality smacked me into a wall.

When you were 14 months old, we had to dash you to the hospital. Your body was working overtime to get a breath, with an unbreakable fever of 104°. And you were so lethargic. A rag-doll version of your normally plucky self.

Limp with pain, looking up at me with swollen eyes, weeping "Save me!"

I was breaking up and dizzy from the overwhelming terror of the unknown.

Later that day, when you were finally able to get some rest and the worry for you had left me barren, thoughts of pending work deadlines crept into my mind. While I tried to suppress them, the new worries scooted the current ones aside...momentarily. While I listened to the rapid rhythms of your breathing, I was thinking about how this emergency came about at the wrong time, as if one can plan for emergencies. Work was crazy.

Your sharp coughing spasm snapped me back to the moment. As I caressed your back, my thoughts of work stopped short — *what the hell am I thinking*?!? My daughter is going through the most traumatic time in her life and I'm worrying about how I'm going to meet mounting deadlines, as if the world will implode if I don't get to those projects.

Understand that it has taken me nearly three decades to learn this lesson, so it is not easy to discuss.

Please take a step back every now and again to reflect on your life and your career and make sure they are what you want them to be. Know that you always have the power to change direction and keep the balance. Set priorities and let go of the rest.

With all my being, I love you. Thank you for helping me see what really matters.

Love, Mama

Jacquelyn Rardin is still working on eating right and exercising. Some days, she is good. Others, she is downright naughty. And that is OK!

Listen to Your Inner Voice

Ariel Blair

Work: In transition…

Until recently, **Ariel Blair** was a strategy and planning manager for Hewlett-Packard's Imaging and Printing Group in Barcelona, Spain. She had transferred there from her home in Idaho, only to later have her job be "made redundant." Ariel is writing to her friend Ryan, who is eight years old.

DEAR RYAN,

My birthday present to you is simple: Learn to access, listen to, and trust your inner voice.

Sounds simple, yet it is sometimes extremely difficult. The work world has many messages and signals to impose on us. There is always something else to do, another project that your boss needs right away, a coworker who needs your help, or an urgent request to present at a meeting for which you have had inadequate preparation time. I have learned to listen to what is viscerally true for me. This has meant constantly quieting the noise that competes for my attention so I can hear what is deep inside.

Additionally, you will experience distractions that your European-American colleagues will not. Because your skin is dark, as is mine, there are privileges we cannot assume. The richness of your skin color will lead to internal and external pressures related to bias.

Note that I did not use the word race. Race only exists as a social construct. This is critical to remember. In order to listen to yourself, you need to know who you truly are — as opposed to who you are within someone else's social construct.

I have two ways to access my inner voice: Either spending time meditating or writing in a journal. This creates a space for my inner voice to surface.

Here's an example: One Friday, I glanced at the management staff gathered without Peter, our boss, or me in our conference room. Earlier I had heard a rumor of a meeting and been told by Peter that he had not scheduled one. A knot formed in my stomach. Why was I excluded? Inner alarm bells went off.

Later that afternoon, I saw a member of the staff and asked about the meeting. George told me that yes, the staff had met, and he had intentionally not invited me to that meeting and others. I was so angry and frustrated, I did not know if I should cry or tell George off using words not fit for a professional.

My inner voice told me to keep quiet and not to react visibly. A lump in my throat the size of a golf ball now joined the knot in my stomach. Though appearing calm on the outside, inside I was feeling a mix of anger, frustration, sadness and fear.

Unknowingly, George triggered a range of emotions stored inside of me from so many previous subtle injustices. That weekend, I made myself miserable turning the events over and over in my head, raging and questioning why this was happening as though there were some rational explanation. Unfounded worries about being excluded because of my skin color were waves of distraction, overwhelming my ability to use my inner compass.

During our next staff meeting, I could barely speak for fear of expressing the anger lurking just below the surface. I fought with myself trying to find compassion for my colleagues. An opportunity came at the close of our meeting.

Two women from the department had just proposed a workshop on multicultural awareness. After their presentation, I spoke for the first time. "Just a moment, Peter, I have a something to add." With a quiet and slightly shaking voice, I said, "Given the decision to exclude me from meetings about the reorganization where I have value to contribute, I find it ironic to hear workshop goals like 'inclusion' and 'trust' from this staff."

A couple of people across the table looked startled and started to shake their heads. I looked at George, saying, "I was told I was not invited." George responded clearly with "I did say that."

I will never know why George excluded me from those meetings. What I do know is that by knowing what was true for me and giving voice to that truth, I had a significant impact on those who were present. Not only had I made a point of the inappropriate behavior much more powerfully than if I had succumbed to the temptation and yelled at George on Friday afternoon, I also had the opportunity to see that most of my colleagues participated in the exclusion unknowingly. I had wrongly suspected all of them of participating actively.

Listening to the voice inside that told me to be still and hold my tongue on Friday gave me the opportunity, later, to see the suffering present on those faces as their heads shook in disbelief. It gave me a way to forgive my colleagues for the ignorance of their privilege, and to forgive myself for my own deep anger and fear.

In all my everyday experiences, I am mindful of finding real meaning from moments when I am quiet and listening well. Then I can hear not only my inner voice, but also a heartfelt message from a coworker even when it is not explicitly spoken.

Ryan, these moments are the true gifts of listening to your inner voice.

Happy Birthday.

Ariel Blair's mom died with many dreams unfulfilled, because something practical always came first. Ariel then vowed to live each day fully, never missing an opportunity to be happy in the moment, including launching her own firm after leaving HP.

• • •

Inner Voices
Journey Notes from the Gut

The Time for Love Is Now
I'm tired of waiting for that right person or company to recognize the talent that I can offer. I want to reach inside of myself through the muck and mire and live more with love and less with fear. Within love resides trust, faith, hope, peace, equality, and understanding. None of these reside in fear.

I realized not too long ago that God is trying to hit me over the head with a message. The message is that I should follow my dreams and create my own product. If the job market were going well, I would probably do as I have done in the past: "I'm getting so much work that I better take it while the opportunity exists. I'll put my dream on the back burner for now." Well, now it's time to flame up that burner and get going.

— **Paul Buckley,** who lost his job as a creative director when he spoke up after discovering unethical corporate behavior

• • •

Inner Voices
Journey Notes from the Gut

I Wish I Could Speed It Up

Everyone tells me I'm "living the dream." A year off, full pay, benefits. No worries — just fun, fun, fun.

It sure doesn't seem like that.

What it feels like is, is what??? Umm, being cast aside for people who know less than me (but are getting paid more) and who are screwing up all that I worked for in the last year to create. It sucks. Whoopee, I get to go to the gym every day, where I'm not a mom, or a wife. I'm just sort of unemployed.

Yes, this is a gift of time to figure things out — I get that. But some days I still want it back, or I want to kill my ex-boss. What goes around comes around and his is coming…Just not soon enough for me!

I guess all this will pass. I'm trying hard to let the company go, to stop thinking about what could have been and think about what will be. What will be will be great. I just wish it would hurry up and get here!

— **A former Fortune 25 employee,** who was recently let go due to cost-cutting

Just Be You: Always

Marshall Goldsmith

Work: Helps leaders to lead others and to lead happier lives

Marshall Goldsmith has been hailed by business publications as one of today's Top Ten Executive Educators and Top Five Executive Coaches. He's written eighteen books on leadership.

DEAR YET-TO-BE-BORN GRANDCHILDREN,

Greetings from the past!

One of the greatest thinkers in my field (and in my time) was a man named Peter Drucker. I am very lucky. I got to spend a lot of time with Peter. He always encouraged people to ask, "Who is the customer?" before they do anything.

I finally understood the deeper importance of that question when a woman from the *New Yorker* wrote a profile about me.

She spent two months traveling with me, and interviewing my family, my clients, and many of the people who work with me. She then wrote this very long story and published it for 800,000 people to read. This was a little scary, since some of the *New Yorker* profiles can be pretty negative, and I didn't get to read it ahead of time.

I originally thought that my customers in doing this profile should be my clients — the people who pay me to do my work. I thought that maybe I should "be careful of what I say" and try to act appropriate. Maybe I should be careful not to embarrass anyone.

But, as this woman began to follow me around,

I figured out who I wanted to be my "customers" for this profile. It was you, my yet-to-be-born grandchildren. I decided that this profile was a special opportunity for you to get to know me.

I decided to just act like myself. If I had acted like someone who was too careful of what he said, it would have been a story about an imaginary person. And not me. You might not have the chance to know your grandfather.

Your grandmother and I discussed this, since she's in charge of our money. I told her to assume that we were going to lose $150,000 in business because of this profile. I figured that by just acting like me, I might annoy someone who wouldn't want to work with me anymore. I figured that it would be worth the $150,000 to have a brilliant writer spend two months on a story about me (that I could send to you, and hopefully, to your children). I hoped that I wouldn't lose any more money than this!

As it turns out, I was glad that I just acted like me. I received about 300 emails about the profile. They almost all said the same thing — "It sounds just like you!"

My fears about losing business due to this profile were wrong. Not only did I not lose any business, I was later interviewed for the *Harvard Business Review* and many other publications. I now have an eight-month waiting list for new clients.

I learned something from this experience that I would like to share with you: Just be you. Always.

You are good enough. In the long run, any success you achieve, if you don't act like yourself, won't seem real anyway. You will just feel like an imposter or a phony.

In my career, I am sort of a pioneer. I was one of the original developers of something called 360° feedback. I help successful leaders achieve a positive, long-term change in their behavior. I also try to help the people that I work with (and everyone around them) have a happier life.

If I look back upon what I have contributed in my career, my largest contributions have all come from *stuff that I invented myself.* No one can tell you how to do something that hasn't been done before. If you are going to do anything creative, you have to make it up yourself! There is no guidebook.

If you have an idea that sounds good — go for it! Just be you. Do what is in your heart. You may fail, but at least you will have tried.

Don't waste your life worrying too much about being normal. Lots of people are normal. It is more fun to be different. *Just be you.*

When your grandchildren read the story of your life, make sure that it is really about you.

Marshall Goldsmith is a Buddhist whose mission is to help people have happier lives. His personal philosophy is "Be happy now! Life is good."

• • •

Inner Voices
Journey Notes from the Gut

Take Your Work Seriously, Not Yourself
You will have a serious job where people depend on you, but do not take yourself too seriously. Have fun

and play every chance you get. Some folks think play and work are opposites; the opposite of play is actually psychosis. We need play to keep ourselves connected, vital, and sharp — music, games, sports, theater, whatever. Just play, guys!

And it's not about doing something specific — it's probably more important just to be *playful*. Cracking inside jokes, tossing some stuffed fish around, throwing movie dialogue back and forth, making up songs, and just enjoying life will help you make it through tough times.

Marley, Noah, and Joshua, I hope that I have done more in my life than just leave you this list of ideas, values and principles. I hope I have modeled this behavior. And that you do the same for your kids, too.

— **Jody Lentz's** last gig in big business was as Director of Outreach for Executive Discovery, at LEGO Serious Play. He's since joined the ranks of entrepreneurial free agents.

• • •

Face Why You're Here

Mary Zisk

Work: Trying to be the best single mom she can be

Mary Zisk is a graphic designer, and mother to her adopted daughter Anna, and a poodle, a guinea pig, a cockatiel, an aquatic frog, and fish.

DEAR ANNA,

I came to motherhood late, but in the scheme of life

and work, I had to become a mother.

I've always loved my work, and have always put creativity and personal fulfillment ahead of money. And I've seized opportunities when they have come up instead of waiting for "some day." Once I had a job that made me doubt my abilities and creativity. I quit and spent the summer painting in France. I thought I would turn into a new me that summer. I didn't, but I came back stronger and enhanced, willing to face future uncertainties.

After a few years, I sold my apartment and bought a house in the burbs. Finally, my own grass and trees, but I was losing excitement for my work.

Then one day, I watched an Oprah show about finding fulfillment in life, hoping I'd find some enlightenment about my work life. At one point, Oprah asked "Why did God put you on this planet?" and I answered, "To be someone's mother." Wow! Not the answer I expected.

Having passed 40, and not finding my best friend in life to marry, I had thought about single-parent adoption. It was scary. But I knew I couldn't go through life without being a mother.

With my parents' and clients' support, I started an eight-month journey through adoption that took me to Moscow to adopt you, my Anna.

You were already three, loaded with emotional baggage from your impoverished life. But you were also full of love and energy. My intended three-month maternity leave turned into a year. I couldn't bear to take you out of an orphanage to put you right into day care. You had so much catching up to do.

That year at home with you was the hardest work I've ever done! I suddenly had a new respect for stay-at-home moms.

I know it can be tough having a single woman as your mom. You see kids going home at 3 P.M. when you have to stay in the after-school program. Or you envy the kids with two parents who can afford to go to Disney World every year. Or you really miss having a dad. I wish you could have all these things, but this is our reality. I hope you see in me a woman who loves her child and loves her work. I hope you see a woman who wasn't afraid to take chances, who sought to nurture a child and a career. I hope you see that dreams and fulfillment are more important than money.

I still have fears. I worry about this difficult economy and spotty freelance work. I worry about surviving in a field that relies more and more on youth and technology. I worry about having to work just to make money, not to create. I worry about having the physical stamina to work until 65. I worry about having to work past 65. But I've faced fear before.

Anna, listen to your heart and don't be afraid to follow it, whether you open a doggy day care center or join the FBI. I'm always here to be supportive, as my parents were for me.

Love, Mom

Mary Zisk has traveled the world, but her most momentous trip was to Moscow to become a mother. "I'll always remember meeting Anna for the first time in a very dim, crowded airport when she flew in from her hometown of Perm, near the Ural Mountains. At three, she was the size of an eighteen-month-old, with crossed eyes and boyishly short, cropped hair. When we arrived at my host's apartment, I had to strip her down to return all her clothes to the orphanage. I immediately put her into a tub of warm water, but she didn't know to sit down. Once I got her to sit, she giggled and splashed in her first bath! Much more fun than the cool showers she was used to." Mary is author/illustrator of the children's book, *The Best Single Mom in the World: How I Was Adopted.*

• • •

Inner Voices
Journey Notes from the Gut

Know What You Stand For
I truly believe the reason I've only worked for six months at a time at two different jobs during the past two and a half years is because I was not being authentic.

First, I took a job at a place where I never wanted to work — I needed the money. Big mistake. If you don't feel right about a company, you probably don't belong there. I didn't belong. Then, I took a job because I lost faith in myself. Instead of starting my own business, I took a job with a boss who I knew I didn't like. Again, after six months, I was gone.

During my unemployment, I took a long hard look at where I'd been and what I liked and didn't like about myself, the jobs and the people I worked with. I found my passion as soon as I paid attention to what makes me happy. The universe seems to only support your greatest good. I hope the universe supports me in the company I recently started.

— **Tami Belt** spent 13 years in corporate America — including two final attempts that failed because she failed to follow her passion.

Embrace Opportunity, See Potential Everywhere

Jane Puckett

Work: Making a difference in the lives of those she manages, and in the lives of patients everywhere

Jane Puckett's passion for and background in science landed her at Merck & Co., where she is currently Director of Oncology Marketing. She is writing to her daughter, Jessica, age 13. She also has a son, Jeffrey, nine years old.

DEAR JESSICA,

I began my first job as a scientist and always believed I would stay a scientist. In some respects, this is still true, but what I have learned through my experiences is that scientific skills can be applied in many different ways.

I've been an immunologist exploring antibodies in the treatment of infectious diseases. I have also been a microbiologist, investigating new ways to treat infections, and have been fortunate enough to work on two compounds that later became actual products. But over time, I became bored with the monotony of testing compounds in the same way over and over again.

I was approached to become product manager for a new product for hair loss. Hair loss! This wasn't a serious disease — how would I be perceived? Yet, when I studied the depth and integrity of the research, it was staggering! So I worked with key opinion leaders to deliver the scientific and medical messages about this product. I traveled extensively throughout the world supporting medical and scientific programs, symposia, medical congresses, and exhibits. I never worked harder and never felt more energized than I did during those three years!

Then the product launched. That very day, my job became less exciting. I was restless again.

At the same time, my personal life began to change in a very dramatic and tragic way. Your grandmother was diagnosed with pancreatic cancer, and died four months later. Then a coworker and friend died in a plane crash while traveling to a meeting. This became a turning point. I remember boarding a plane soon after and being asked by the flight attendant to identify my next of kin in the event of a tragedy. I thought to myself: "What am I doing? I just lost my mother and a good friend, my children are young and they need their mother..."

For the first time in my career, I seriously considered resigning and taking some time to be with my family. Your dad and I carefully considered the financial aspects of the decision, as well as my emotional needs. Quitting is not something I have ever been good at. I had worked very hard all through school and throughout my career and was very proud of my accomplishments. I was not comfortable with just "giving up."

Then the phone rang...A friend of mine was taking a new position and she was asked to identify successors for her position. Was I interested?

After much deliberation, I took the job — associate director of communications. It's now four years later, and I have moved beyond that position, having been promoted two years ago. I manage a staff of 14 people, and derive enormous benefit from this position. When I first joined the group, everyone was feeling underacknowledged and underappreciated. They felt that the only time they heard feedback was when something went wrong. Now, I'm very proud of how things have changed! The visibility of the group has grown, customer service has improved, and so has our staff morale. I have never regretted my decision to stay, and having survived those difficult times has become my barometer for gauging tough times in my life today.

So, through this 17-year journey I have learned the following lessons that I hope will one day be meaningful to you:

- **Embrace opportunity** and see the potential in each new experience. You never know when or where a new opportunity may present itself. Change is good, it is how we grow and develop.

- **Be true to yourself.** Never compromise your values or morals for the good or advancement of your position. Be honest and genuine in all that you do.

- **Work hard and play hard.** Regardless of what you do, do it with conviction, passion, and pride — this is how excellence is achieved! Also strive for balance in your life. Don't give up your hobbies and the things you love to do because of work. These diversions will sustain and nurture you when work fatigue sets in.

- **Prioritize** what is most important in your life. Don't abandon your family and friends as you pursue your professional goals. Important people in your life will support and love you during difficult times in your career, and motivate and inspire you to succeed.

Always remember these lessons, and you will be whatever and whoever you want to be. I can't wait to see how your great adventure turns out!

I love you, Mom

In her former life, **Jane Puckett** was a softball pitcher, a trumpet player in a marching band, and a scuba diver.

• • •

You Are Who You Choose to Be

Dennis Bonilla

Work: Leads others, keeping the human condition in mind

Dennis Bonilla is CEO and president of Medsn, a medical education and marketing communications company.

DEAR ASHLEY JENNIFER,

My granddaughter,
To be opened on the celebration of your 21st year…
   If life were not so full of unexpected events, I would have written this letter years ago, for your

mother — my daughter, Jennifer — who graced us for only 21 years, but has been a continual inspiration for me. It then would have made its way to your gentle hands from hers, with some humorous additions, anecdotes, and wisdom she would have gained throughout her business career. But it was not meant to happen in that manner. So I hope that as you read these words from Grandpa, it will bring to you a smile.

First, you should know that your mom certainly had a knack for work from a very early age. I remember when I had opened a few restaurants as a sideline business. At the age of ten, she would come in on weekends to play hostess and cashier. She was always great at client schmoozing, and an ace money-handler.

One time, she pleaded her case for getting minimum wage from me, instead of an allowance plus the additional few bucks I gave her under the table. I took that moment to teach her the cruel concept of federal and state withholding taxes, and the inherent value of free employee meals. She quickly did the math in her head and opted for underground funds plus all the chicken fingers and fries she could eat.

I have been working now for 30 years. From submarines, to nuclear power plants, to high technology software, and to healthcare education. Yet throughout it all, one fundamental principle keeps repeating itself: The need for managers and executives to understand that the human condition is the foundation for all long-term success in the brutal, hostile business world.

This revelation did not come overnight. At first, my primal urge was to succeed using all reasonable and legal means. After all, there was a family to feed.

Work is a juggling act between challenges and aspirations. We all want to live up to our personal standards and values, be fair to the people who work for us, lend a hand to people in need, earn the respect of our families and friends, and above all, maintain our personal integrity. We must also meet the expectations of our customers and shareholders (often in the face of relentless profit pressures) — and maintain the foundation of our families' security.

Usually, we find ways to juggle these different challenges and aspirations. Sometimes, we find we can't. At that point, the stakes can be very high. They go to the heart of what it means to be a successful leader/manager and a decent, responsible human being.

As you move into the workplace, and possibly lead other people, I would suggest that you answer five urgent questions:

- How should I think and act when faced with defining moments?
- How do I resolve them in ways I can live with?
- Do I think I can lead/manage innocently?
- Who am I?
- What is my moral center?

When I chose not to answer these questions, or not to adhere to my own principles, I regretted it dearly. I still recall with deep sadness my decision to relocate for a company when your mom was a teenager. I moved away from my family for a job. I knew it was wrong, yet rationalized it so I could live with myself.

Astonishingly enough, sensing my anguish, six months later your mom decided to come live with me for a few years to make sure I was OK, and not lonely. She was amazingly intuitive and compassionate for such a young girl.

Never again did I discount my inner voice.

Ashley, you are not what society and randomness have made you; you are what you have chosen to be. How we act and respond to those polarities is where we separate greatness from mediocrity. Managing polarity teaches us there are no solutions, only changes in attitude. What matters is not what you end up choosing, but *how*. The *how* is what gives you character.

Some people will be more talented than you, some will be smarter than you. But you have the capacity to be great. Greatness comes with recognizing that your potential is limited only by how you choose, how you use your freedom, how resolute you are, how persistent you are, and by your attitude.

Ashley, we are all free to choose our attitude. What will your choices be after today?

All my love, Grandpa Dennis

P.S. If you need a consultant at any time, call me. Of course, like your mom, I would expect unlimited chicken fingers as part of any compensation package.

If you ask **Dennis Bonilla**, he'll tell you he's really a musician and a tennis player. Unfortunately, his skills in those areas were not commercially viable beyond college level. He loves to fly his airplane along the California coastline. But his newest, biggest joy is his year-old daughter, Sophia Lillian.

Speak Your Truth

Nancy Adler

Work: Helps others see what's beneath their professional façades

Nancy J. Adler is a professor of International Management at McGill University in Montreal, Canada. She has written over 100 articles and several books on global leadership, and was the first person in Canada to be selected to become a Fellow of both the Academy of International Business and the Academy of Management. She's writing to both of her great-grandmothers.

Vienna, February 5, 1939: *Valiantly trying to keep the cascade of tears from erupting across their faces, Laura and Nina pleaded with their children to board the train with the four precious tickets and hard-gotten passports. They begged them to escape so the family might live. The train pulled out of Vienna with Laura's and Nina's married son and daughter and their two children (including Liselotte, my then 14-year-old mother-to-be) aboard. The clandestine escape led the family from Austria through Zurich, London, and New York, and then ultimately on to California. Although already in their eighties, Laura and Nina hid and survived for five years before the Nazis murdered them, Nina at Treblinka and Laura in Auschwitz.*

DEAREST LAURA AND NINA,

How do I thank you for the ultimate sacrifice? You died so that I might be born. How will I ever be able to understand that anyone could love me so much before I was even born, before I was able to earn your love or anyone else's?

I know from the stories my mother told me that, in the ultimate act of courage and love, you demanded that your children (my grandparents) escape, even though it meant leaving you behind to face the cruelest of deaths.

How, in the day-to-day reality of my safe and privileged North American life, do I honor your names?

"Nancy, you have to speak your truth,
for if not, we will have died in vain."

When did I first hear your voices? Lovingly supporting me, yet also demanding that I speak my truth. What truth do I have that could possibly be worthy of your sacrifice?

No, that's the wrong question. If I have learned anything from your story, it is that love and courage are given to each of us; they are not earned.

Shaped by love and courage, the only honest question is: What truth is mine to tell?

I know I'll never know the whole answer, but I am beginning to understand that you have been there with me many times, including at work, when your love demanded that I speak the truth and your courage supported me in doing so.

I remember the first time I decided to invite the executives in a global leadership seminar to escape their well-worn biographies of success and to share stories about their most courageous moments at work. The stories transformed each of us: We could no longer view one another as merely global finance, strategy, marketing, and human resource executives without standing in awe of our collective humanity.

I know now that you were there in the Women's Leadership Forum when Amal, a Lebanese woman executive, burdened with the undeserved guilt of having been forced to watch terrorists murder her childhood friend, revealed the weight of her until-that-moment life-defining question: "Why did I live instead of my friend?" With your support, I knew to insist that she change her question to "With the gift of my life and my friend's love, what am I meant to offer the world?"

Not surprisingly, Amal, whose very name means *hope*, has gone on to make highly significant contributions to her organization and the world.

And yes, I know you were there when I demanded that a recently raped Canadian executive, rather than giving up and returning to psychiatric care, answer the question, "What has this awful experience of shame and pain taught me about leadership?" The insights that emerged from Maire-Claire's struggle are among the most moving and profound I have ever read. Not long after our conversation, Marie-Claire boarded a plane for England to assume regional responsibility for her company's European expansion. Her psychiatrists still claim it was a miracle.

Laura and Nina, you were the miracle.

Without you standing there with me, I would have stayed within the bounds of normal management-seminar discussions, never daring to see, let alone address, the pains, fears, and aspirations hiding beneath our ever so thinly disguised professional façades.

Yesterday I confronted a seemingly very self-assured Italian advertising executive, telling him: "Guido, my fear for you is not that you won't succeed, you will. My fear is that you will do nothing that gives you personal meaning; You will succeed at someone else's life."

Rather than rejecting my seemingly inappropriate infringement on his private life, Guido quietly, yet publicly, with all his colleagues looking on, murmured, "That's exactly my fear."

Laura and Nina, it was you, wasn't it, who insisted that I say yes to giving that keynote address to the Arab bankers' conference in Abu Dhabi, just weeks after September 11th, while all my friends insisted that it was too dangerous, especially for a Jewish American woman?

Of course it was, and it was you who guided me, with lots of help from my Muslim friends, to write my entire global leadership speech based on Koranic injunctions to recognize, respect, and honor diversity.

How else would I have understood that that was my moment to speak to the world about the love, respect, and courage demanded today of any true leader?

I haven't been so nervous in years about any speech.

And remember the 13th-century poem by Rumi that I — or should I say *we* — closed with:

The breezes at dawn have secrets to tell you
Don't go back to sleep!
You must ask for what you really want
Don't go back to sleep!
People are going back and forth
Across the doorsill where the two worlds touch,
The door is round and open,
Don't go back to sleep!

Laura and Nina, they applauded endlessly, and then invited me back to the United Arab Emirates. Just last month I returned from Dubai; if they only knew they had invited all three of us back.

These last few years I have grown increasingly less interested in continuing to publish traditional academic books and articles, the bread-and-butter of a successful university and consulting career.

My urge is to speak about issues and feelings that no longer fit into the dehydrated language of management; that are no longer reducible to an endless parade of footnotes.

Not surprisingly, my ideas are increasingly born on the canvases of my paintings, long before they emerge into articulate rows marching across book pages and speech galleys.

Was it you who gave me the courage to accept the invitation to become an artist-in-residence at the Banff Centre, rather than spending my sabbatical, as everyone had expected me to, working on some neatly circumscribed research project within an all-too familiar university?

Of course it was.

Art is my truth; offering it to the world hopefully fulfills your dream for me.

Dearest Laura and Nina, I can't erase history, but hopefully I can honor your names. Hopefully, with your love and courage supporting me, I can be one more voice connecting us through our profound humanity across all the divides of culture, language, religion, ethnicity, and nationality that have tried so hard to extinguish our ability to live peacefully together and share the planet.

Sent with profound love,
Nance
Your Great-Granddaughter

Nancy J. Adler consults with major global corporations and organizations worldwide. She is also an artist, working primarily in watercolors and ink, media she says "that you can't control, you can only dance with." Recently she painted her images of Bach's and Sibelius's violin concerti, with live orchestra, as the opening and closing plenary at global leadership conferences at Borl Castle and in her mother's home city, Vienna.

DISCOVERY

FINDING THE LESSONS TO BE LEARNED, THE QUESTIONS TO BE ASKED

"Don't kiss tush,
and beware carnivorous sheep."

• • •

"Honey, there are no short cuts!"

• • •

"Curiosity is the most powerful tool you have."

• • •

"Most of what matters
comes from our deepest values."

Like these work diarists, you have a lifetime of hard-won wisdom. And you've spent years figuring out what to ask when tough choices are thrown at you. But it's easy to forget all that when confronted with the daily

pressures in today's *morebetterfaster*
workloads.

• • •

My research shows that most of us
jump right into triage mode —
checking things off our list
without reflecting on all that we
already know.
Much of our own wisdom
gets forgotten and trampled
in the daily rush.

• • •

It's time to remember.

• • •

What made your greatest
work experience so great?
What made your worst experience so bad?
What is the most important
thing missing from your life right now?
Who is most important to you?
What lesson has served you best
throughout your career?
What message has been bouncing
inside your head for the past year?
Who influenced you the most?

• • •

Allow the letters in this section to
get you started on questions like these.

The Top Ten for Women

Linda Stone

Work: Envisioning the future of attention, connection, and community

In April 2002 **Linda Stone** left Microsoft, where she was vice president for Corporate and Industry Initiatives, reporting to CEO Steve Ballmer. Seven weeks after leaving to pursue projects of her own, she lost her home in a fire. "How had I come to this place?" she wondered. "From a thousand miles an hour one minute to being homeless, with neighbors bringing me blankets and clothing the next. I remember how touched I was when friends brought flowers and plants. The powerful contrast between the burned-out, smoky structure that was my house and the stunning, sweet-smelling roses kept my imagination and spirit intact. In the last two years, I've moved seven times. Now, finally back in my rebuilt home, I am taking slow, confident steps forward again. Re-engaging." She dedicates this letter to the many who filled her life with love and laughter.

TO ALL THE WOMEN I'VE COACHED AND MENTORED,

Your courage, passion, and persistence touch me. I've been blessed with mentors and I'm glad to be there for you through many of your challenging times and times of growth. There are so many things that we, as women working in large corporations, seem to have in common in our struggle.

The first is a dangerous one. Often in corporate life, our drive and desire to excel take over and we put our bodies and our relationships on the delayed maintenance plan. It doesn't work for our cars, and it certainly doesn't work for us.

I was so completely seduced by the excitement, the adventure, the possibilities. I often forgot I had a body, forgot that that body had limits, and relied,

sometimes too much, on the patience and loyalty
of friends as I traveled and worked too many late
nights, showed up late or not at all for social
gatherings when work demands pulled me off center.
By now, I've forgotten most of the important projects
and deadlines that kept me at the office so late at
night. I have not forgotten taking Joey to the
Winchester Mystery House for a school report, going
to Abe and Zoe's soccer games and music recitals, or
flying to L.A. for Max's plays.

The opportunity here is to set boundaries
around the time we spend working and to schedule
work-outs, time with family, vacations and sleep. If
we don't respect ourselves enough to take care of our
bodies, minds, spirits, why should anyone else grant
us the respect we feel we deserve?

Why work so hard for so many years? Is it all
about being able to pay for first-rate medical help in
order to survive whatever is left?

I didn't heed the loving warnings of friends and
mentors on this front, and have been on a long road
back to better health. I'll get there, and, at the same
time, I hope that my hard-learned lesson that delayed
maintenance is not a great choice will help you not
have to suffer in the same way.

For many women, power and exertion are
related. I've come to believe in the truth of this
anonymous quote: "Power is not having to make
sense to be believed. Powerlessness is not being
believed no matter how much sense you make."

Also, as women, we are more inclined to take
things personally, creating all kinds of stories around

situations that impair our ability to see the facts. By making it personal, we can wind up having a lot more drama in our lives than is productive.

The Buddhists have a great way of looking at this. Notice it, but don't be attached. When we notice ourselves creating a story, we have an opportunity to take a step back, observe ourselves, and let the story dissolve. We can focus instead on what outcome we are working toward. If we can stay out of the story, we can move forward in a more productive way for ourselves and for the organization.

On this journey, one of the most powerful tools we have is our curiosity. Whenever we feel defensive, hurt, personally attacked, confused, or afraid, we have a choice — we can get very curious. Rather than saying, "I never would have said that," we can say, "I wonder what these people heard me say? I wonder what their perception is?"

People often ask me if it is important to create long-range plans in order to climb the corporate ladder. Some of my peers are committed to five-year plans. I've never had one. I've always followed my passions and interests and things have unfolded. This can be balanced with a long-term plan as long as you stay tuned in to opportunities.

Studies show that it doesn't matter whether you create plans or make it up as you go along using your passions. The results are the same. For those of us with strengths in the area of innovation, following our passions is key. For those with strengths in procedural thinking, planning is both comforting and helpful.

My top ten rules for women:

1. **Engage in activities that show self-respect.**
Take care of yourself with sleep, exercise, nutrition, schedule. If you don't, no one else will. If you're willing to work around the clock, your peers and superiors will always expect that of you, and you'll find yourself in a pattern that's challenging to shift. One woman I coached argued that she only needed four to five hours of sleep a night. After months of coaching, she made time for more sleep. "Linda, I can't believe how much better everything is with eight hours of sleep! This was so simple. Almost too simple."

2. **Don't take it personally.**

3. **Curiosity is the most powerful tool you have.**
Curiosity is more powerful than a good defense.

4. **We can use our will in many ways.** Will can be used to "push through" or it can be used for greater attunement and awareness. Pushing through will ultimately use every last drop of your energy. Using your will for awareness will support you in maintaining balance.

5. Stories are good for books and movies. They serve to create drama, confusion, and distraction at work. A **focus on facts and desired outcomes,** on staying in the moment, can keep us on a productive path.

6. **Your passion can inform and energize you.**

7. "In school, first you get the lesson, then the test. In life, it's **first the test, then the lesson.**"

8. **Learning is a vitamin.**

9. **Attention is your scarcest resource.**

Use it with intention.

10. **Trust your intuition.** If you overrule it, it will send out stronger and more painful warnings.

With love, Linda

Linda Stone is now focused on her own creative projects, writing, speaking, and consulting. She is also on the National Board of the World Wildlife Fund and involved with the Philanthropic Collaborative for Integrative Medicine. Over the past two decades, she has been recognized as one of the top 100 leaders in today's digital revolution.

• • •

Inner Voices
Journey Notes from the Gut

Be True, and Love Yourself Unconditionally

Seven years before my retirement, I had an epiphany. I was driving home from work thinking about, of all things, unconditional love. I started making a mental list of all the people in my life — friends, family, co-workers — who loved me unconditionally. It was a long list, and the most amazing thing was that everyone I needed to be on it was there — except me.

I asked myself *Why?* The answer: "Because you're not good enough." It occurred to me in that moment that by not loving myself, I was dishonoring all the people who had freely chosen to love me. If my family and friends and coworkers loved me in spite of — or perhaps even because of — my imperfections, wasn't it high time for me to accept myself as is, just as they did — warts and all?

That day I embarked on a new love affair with me. I finally decided that I was, indeed, good enough.

Everything in my life changed after that day. I made peace with myself and came to know real contentment. My work life changed drastically, too... for the better. I began to take risks because I believed in myself. I wasn't afraid of disapproval, and that allowed my creativity to surface. When I focused on pleasing myself instead of others, my anxiety evaporated. I started doing really good work and was more successful than ever. The difference was that now I believed that I deserved that success.

— When **Sue Brooks** retired from Bank of America, she moved from contentment to *joy*. She's newly married and living in Vermont, where she loves herself, and her husband, *unconditionally*.

• • •

Anything Is Possible. If...

Neal Sofian

Work: Telling stories, and giving them the space to make a difference

Neal Sofian is the CEO of the NewSof Group — using the Web to build communities for people with health issues like cancer and arthritis, as well as corporate clients. He's writing to his kids, Rachael, age 13, and Noah, 18.

DEAR RACHAEL AND NOAH,

Sometimes we can only see the path that we have taken when we look back to wonder how we got where we are.

You have heard about my jobs before you were born: Working on a sheep ranch, and at the cemetery, owning a snow-cone machine with a rabbi in a head shop, doing stand-up comedy, and even those two endless years of working for state government. What they have in common is that they have provided me a treasure trove of stories. Here is one you haven't heard.

Everyday People (EDP) was a pretty crazy place. Your mother and I did crisis and suicide intervention, emergency housing, runaway youth counseling, drug identification, drug and alcohol counseling. Those we helped ranged from the confused, to wonderful folks on their way to other places, to the bizarre. We dealt with pretty much anyone who didn't fit into, or had been tossed out of, the social service system. Everyday People was an anti-establishment drug-crisis service agency and proud of it.

On my first night as executive director, the volunteers had just staged a coup, and were voting to close down the agency. I was sitting on a legless couch that reeked of sweat, puke, and who knows what, wondering how I could possibly have gotten myself into this. I didn't know these people, had no background in drug or alcohol counseling, and was devoid of a staff or money.

I convinced three of the volunteers to stay on, and the four of us decided we could keep the place operating twenty-four hours a day, seven days a week. We were young and didn't know this was ridiculous.

Unlike other agencies, EDP refused to provide the names and social security numbers of our clients to the state funding agencies so we could get reimbursed for our drug and alcohol counseling. Which was why we were broke. The previous director had a brilliant solution, but hadn't yet put it in place: The volunteers could identify themselves as receiving counseling, substituting for our real clients. We could get funding and our clients could keep their anonymity. I decided to make it happen.

We were able to get over 40 volunteers to agree to sign up for "counseling." Then the volunteer staff delivered services to our clientele. Everything we said in contract with the state actually happened, just for a different set of people.

Believe it or not, this worked for almost a year before the state agencies got wise to us. We had done everything we said we would do, though not the way the state had in mind. Besides, we were providing services to hundreds of people more cost-effectively than any other social service in the city. As a result, the city came up with additional funds, and we were able to grow the organization to having eight paid (I use the term lightly) staff and a hundred volunteers.

Everything seemed to be going great. Even the police were quietly supporting us. After all, we dealt with many of the same folks, and having us around meant they had an alternative to jail for the strange cases. Less paperwork for them. We were odd bedfellows, the freaks and the cops, but it worked.

Then, something horrible happened. One of our clients raped and murdered a runaway girl who was staying with us. The newspapers were all over it. There was a half-page picture of me under the

headline "Girl Murdered at Everyday People."
There were calls for us to close the place down. Even
though we were an effective agency, we looked and
acted different. Our neighbors were afraid, and
wanted us gone.

Though there was a public inquiry, the biggest
questions we asked were of ourselves. Were we really
doing something beneficial for the community? Were
we the right people to be doing this? We were okay
with putting ourselves out of business, but only if our
unique service was not needed. We faced down the
possibility of EDP ending. Others agreed. The city,
the police, and most of the social service community
came to our defense and continued to fund us.

From that time on, at the core of our training,
we would tell the stories of how we got our funding,
the murder, and the beliefs we have about our clients,
and the way we went about our work. And there
were many more stories about the weird people and
situations we encountered. During every training
session, we announced to the new trainees that if
the day came when we weren't meeting our clients'
needs, we would close ourselves down. It was
through these stories that our culture was shared
with each new group of volunteers.

After four years, I was totally cooked. Leaving
EDP felt as if I was leaving my family and going out
on my own. Those years taught me lessons that I take
everywhere, including:

- **Anything is possible if I really believe** my work is
  more important than just me, and I am willing
  to take extraordinary steps to make things happen.

- It's easy to rebel against the rules, but it is more fun and effective to **turn them on their head** and use them to my advantage.
- **It's the people I care about,** and who care about me, who will help me through the hardest things in life. Some of these people may not be whom I would expect. I have to remember to value and seek out people different than me. It isn't always easy and it's almost always a good thing.
- **Community matters.**
- The best way to share our beliefs and work has been **through the stories we tell,** from generation to generation of staff. These stories became the basis of learning and applying ideas to new situations. They are at the heart of innovation. Now they are my business.
- **I might as well be myself** because people are going to find out anyway.

I look at the two of you and see endless possibilities. You both have so much talent and that twinkle in your eye that encourages others to follow you. I hope you listen to the stories your mom and I tell you, and use those that can help you make your own way. Then do what in your heart you know is right. It will serve you well.

Love,
Dad

Neal Sofian is also a clay artist and would never be mistaken as the president of the Hair Club for Men.

Count Your Blessings and Dance!

Dee Cook

Work: Mostly focused on just living, and enjoying all that life has to offer

Dee Cook spent 20 years as an executive in multiple corporate and nonprofit businesses. Recently, one week after her husband fell victim to a corporate restructuring, Dee discovered she may well have to battle cancer a second time. She is writing to her three children: Jennifer, who owns an ice cream parlor, single mom Melissa, and construction firm owner Jonathan.

DEAR CHILDREN,

My father, a white-collar businessman, discovered he had cancer of the larynx at age 38. Daddy was a very special human being, who accepted his condition, and passed on to me a work-related lesson that I'd like to pass on to you: It's all about how we drive on our journey. Here's mine...

Since Daddy's speech deteriorated after surgery, he couldn't go back to his old career, and worked the remainder of his work life in a steel mill. He would not allow his coworkers to feel sorry for him. He used to tell me how simple and uncomplicated life becomes when we treasure our speech. When you must train yourself to speak with limited air and muscle control, you choose words wisely — words are fewer and more meaningful.

To help carry the financial load, Mom worked evenings and weekends at the telephone company. That is, until she was in a serious car accident, and was diagnosed with cancer while Daddy was dealing with a series of heart attacks. From her faith, perseverance and courage I learned: *Our body, mind, and spirit can be their own unique healers when we let them.* She showed me the way!

My brother is a dark thread in my tapestry reminding me of the consequences of greed. He served no one but himself even unto Mom's passing. He taught me to *beware of those who seek to rise or acquire at someone else's expense.* And never to take credit for someone else's work; eventually you will be defined by your lack of integrity. In the end it WILL catch up with you, and cost you your career dreams and relationships. *Never do it!*

My grandmother (Nana) was my rock. We walked to church together every Sunday. She taught me reverence. She was a simple and very wise person who treated servanthood as a privilege. She understood boundaries, appropriate behavior, and gratitude. She taught me many valuable lessons. Among them are:

It could be worse.

This, too, shall pass.... and...

Count your blessings!

There have been moments in all the years that followed when I've felt I didn't measure up to Nana's wisdom, and believed the world was judging our lifestyle and me. During my first marriage, while enduring affairs, abuse, noninvolvement, greed, and downright self-centeredness, I experienced the worst of the '80s working ethos: Rapid-track success went to my ex's head. He wanted more fun, more money, and less commitment.

I have always believed that our trials and challenges are part of the training so we become better prepared — cultivating compassion and understanding, and eliminating excuses.

Now, your choices will influence your destiny; don't blame anyone else; not your parents, not the conditions of your childhood, and certainly not your colleagues and peers. (Notice I said *influence,* not *determine.* Mistakes are a part of the process.) Some of my mistakes created lessons learned for me to pass on to you:

Entitlement is not an option.

Earn your income!

After nine years of me being single and the only breadwinner, in 1990, *we,* as a family, remarried. Don and I shared a common value system (family first), and had both been deeply scarred by previous marriages. You know, all too well, that this didn't mean life would finally be perfect.

Last year, Dad (not your biological father, but, as you have pointed out, Don is a first-class dad) and I bought our first home together, as well as a sailboat. This after a decade of job relocations built on false promises, a real estate deal gone bad that wiped us out financially, getting children through college, weddings, deaths and births, having the courage to pick up and leave two successful jobs in New York to return to help care for elderly parents, rebuilding careers, heart problems for Dad, surgery that saved me from paralysis from a car accident, followed by breast cancer.

We did it! With all our training, we were able to

conquer the '90s. Now you know why we named our boat VICTORI-US.

So, who are we anyway? What really matters? The lesson learned that had to be unlearned is that things and people don't define you. Less is actually more. Stay uncluttered, physically and emotionally.

Eventually, we discover that all those things we once resented played a pivotal role in our growth. No one grows in a comfort zone. You can't save the world, but you can contribute to its wellness. Build yourself up so you can give back.

These are tough times we live in. Our story is like everyone else's today; we just got there first.

I am so proud of you. I am, indeed, blessed!

I hope you dance!

However you choose to do it, you'll be OK. The lessons were learned well.

Since writing this letter, **Dee Cook** and her husband had to "seriously re-group," as she says. Between medical crises and unemployment, "We had to downsize everything within 60 days, selling most everything we own, and moving several states away just to survive. However, I am convinced these times are made to make us, not break us. We're moving to another victory."

• • •

Inner Voices
Journey Notes from the Gut

I Must Get Accustomed to Uncertainty

I've been in this job for a year. I still feel in transition. It seems that no job will ever again feel secure. I will always be on edge. Perhaps September 11th has changed my perspective forever. Perhaps it is the culture change in my new situation, or because I am now a consultant without a permanent workplace or phone number.

How do I get comfortable with constant change and uncertainty? I am qualified, productive, and effective. I add value to the firm and the projects. I must get accustomed to uncertainty.

— **Marie,** who was displaced a year ago and is in a new job

• • •

Beware the Perils of Carnivorous Sheep

Melissa Gessner

Work: Creates wonders with words and images

Melissa Gessner has made her living in advertising for the last decade. In other incarnations, she has worked as a creative planner, journalist, and political strategist. She's writing to a friend who turned to her for help in dealing with an emotionally abusive manager.

DEAR JANET,

This business has been fairly good to me, as I hope it will be to you. It's also driven me witless at times because I can't be content in leaving the work at the office and letting "good enough" be just that. That's the nature of creative work, I suppose. If you really want to make this your profession, there are things to remember that might save you some frustration along the way....

Always roll with the punches. And honey, there'll be a lot of punches. That means you'll have to learn how to punch back, and discern when to punch and when it's better to roll. In the agencies of the "old-guard" network you will have to work harder, stay longer, and earn less than most of your male colleagues. Often talent or even competence (in either gender) are not necessarily criteria for advancement. Know it, understand it, and don't think about it again.

Don't expect everyone to share your vision. Sometimes they won't even have a vision. If you are lucky enough to have one, then have the courage and the passion to fight for it. Just know you might not always succeed, and that's alright, too.

The kids you didn't like from high school are still around, and many of them work in advertising. There are also some really wonderfully talented people. You will have to work with all of them, so try to have an open mind. Find something to like about everyone and hold on to that. Hitler liked dogs. Perhaps young Stalin had a pony. Lucrezia Borgia was good at chemistry. Dig deep; you can do it.

Don't kiss tush. In any business there are a number of frustrated proctologists who believe the care of a boss's derriere is the surest way to the top. Disgusting to watch, worse when people start doing it to you and something for which I've never had the stomach. Console yourself that what you may lose in the easy promotion, you'll save in breath mints — and your self-respect.

Seek out people you respect and learn all you can from them. The people you may come to respect may not necessarily be the ones most rewarded and revered by the organization.

Beware carnivorous sheep. This is a business built on manipulating and creating idealized versions of reality. Many of the people you will encounter have mastered this on a personal level as well, so be careful in whom you put your trust. The idea thief, the evil genius, the manipulative climber, plus a few more you'll discover on your own. Be optimistic, but be prudent. It hurts to discover that the little lamb you've been pushing for promotion has suddenly developed a taste for your flesh, and the view from your window office.

Listen to lots of music. It keeps things in perspective. There are few things Miles Davis, David Byrne, The Clash and I can't handle together.

Realize there are more important things in life. I realized all perspective was lost when I missed my mother's 65th birthday to work late on a project that was going out the next morning. The right thing to do was just walk out. Of course, the meeting for which all the sacrifice was necessary was postponed to the following week. I will never get over missing that time with my mother. She has never mentioned it, and we celebrated later in the week — a very poor substitute for a moment lost.

Ultimately, the project was an award-winner, and the little statuette shoved to the back of my bookshelf serves as a constant reminder of the human bankruptcy of my decision.

Never fall in love at or with the work. Both are guaranteed to break your heart.

Find something of value in everything you do. Some of the best projects bring the biggest headaches and the best rewards. It's up to you to decide which you'll carry around with you.

Remember too, I'm always here for you, kiddo.

Fondly, Melissa

Melissa Gessner has an overwhelming fondness for dogs and shoes, both of which she tends to accumulate. Taking in both lost souls and lost soles, she sometimes finds one in the other.

• • •

Learning to Show Up Is Invaluable

Barbara Simonetti

Work: Helps global corporations nurture their networks of people

Barbara Simonetti began her career as a recreational therapist, focused on the healthcare needs of the young and old. She is now an independent consultant in Brookline, Massachusetts, designing corporate meetings that "use all the minds in the room." She is writing to her lifelong friend, Honey, about their first job together.

DEAR HONEY,

Just before we met, I had had two jobs that influenced my perspective on work. In the spring of my senior year in high school, I took a part-time job as an inventory control clerk in a department store. Every day after school, I traveled from the North Bronx to

41st Street in Manhattan, where I sat in front of rows of narrow drawers filled with gridded inventory cards. My job was to take the little white perforated sections of price tags that the sales clerks had torn off socks, underwear, belts, and handbags that they had sold, and sort them by codes into their respective drawers. I then recorded, with hash marks, everything that had been sold.

This could have been really mind-numbing, except that I struck up a relationship with the buyer who shared the office. I'd ask her what a particular item was and alerted her when something was selling fast. She began to teach me about the garment business and ask my opinion on fashion items she was considering buying for the store. This was quite ironic, since I would arrive in my school uniform and by summer was alternating the only two outfits I had. I soon became the buyer's pet project. By September, I went off to college with a fantastic wardrobe all bought at cost off the racks of some of the best showrooms in New York.

I learned that you can make even a really boring job interesting if you assert yourself. And that you can build relationships and learn things at work that are as valuable as your paycheck, or more so.

The next spring, I applied for what I thought was a similar job near my college. I was shocked when the company required I be bonded, have a physical exam with their doctor, submit to a background check, and carry my belongings in a clear purse so they would know if I tried to steal anything. We were closely supervised, not allowed to talk, and

required to punch a time clock for lunch and
bathroom breaks. After three days, I quit. I wanted
work that would nourish my soul, not eat it alive.

Within a week, I found a job at the Police
Athletic League — and with the job came you.

Remember when we first met as PAL Playstreet
Directors in the South Bronx? Remember how tired
we were every night, and how we could still hear the
children calling our names long after we left the block?

What a way to spend our summer! Our office
consisted of an inner-city street, barricaded to traffic,
transformed into a playground — complete with
shuffleboard, basketball, knock hockey, board games,
arts and crafts, a music specialist, a pool (a sprinkler
cap attached to an open fire hydrant) and, oh yeah, a
few packs of stray dogs and resident junkies. Our
supply room was a roach- and rat-infested basement,
and our job was to run a recreation program for
anyone who showed up.

We were both too young and too idealistic to
even think about being afraid of being the only white
women in this "ghetto."

Only a few miles from our homes, we had to
learn a new culture and even a new language — when
I mentioned that "my old man" was picking me up
after work, the kids were disappointed when my
father showed up instead of my boyfriend!

I believe it was on those streets that we first
learned how important it is to be ourselves, yet also
to learn the culture and language of the people we
work with. I carry that lesson into every consulting
project I do. I hear it echoing in my favorite advice to

new facilitators and trainers: "You have to pick people up where they live if you want them to come to your party and dance with you." And I see it in you — that particular genius you have for getting inside the heart of even the sickest or most frightened child.

How lucky we were to be accepted and allowed to be part of life on those streets — the joys and sorrows, the block parties and shootings. We got to use everything we had to make a difference in those kids' lives, and in so doing, to make a difference in our own lives.

I think this is how we learned to "show up" every day at work: All of us — mind and body, heart and soul. It was where we learned how soul-satisfying it can be to help someone else grow and succeed. How important it is to be trusted and appreciated, and to go home knowing that you have used yourself well.

It is also where we first learned that a trusted friend who will help you sort through it all — success and failure — is more valuable than anything. It was exhilarating, and judging from what we have both done the last 35 years, it seems to have been addictive.

Here's to our continued journey!
Barbara

While **Barbara Simonetti** took a career turn away from recreational therapy, her friend, Honey, continued that path. She is now the head of a therapy program at Beth Israel Hospital in New York, where she does extraordinary work with children with brain tumors. "I often call her the Bronx Mother Teresa," says Barbara.

Enjoy the Journey, There Are No Shortcuts

Michael Civitelli and Janet Scarborough

Work: Making the skies and careers safe for people to travel

Michael Civitelli is Manager of Airport Operations at Seattle Tacoma International Airport. **Janet Scarborough** is the head of her own career development firm. They are writing to their 14-month-old son, Alec.

DEAR ALEC,

Your mother and father are usually fiercely opinionated people, but we found ourselves strangely muddled and inarticulate when we sat down to write to you our thoughts about work.

Whenever you do read this: We want you to know that most of the simplistic clichés you'll hear like "Follow your bliss," and "Make a difference in the world," are unhelpful when you are faced with everyday realities and decision-making.

We suspect that our advice will sound old-fashioned and out-of-vogue. We are the type of people who are often told that we are so lucky to have built careers that we love. We silently chuckle because luck had nothing to do with it. Our careers have been built on a great deal of commitment, hard work, and persistence, even when work was not fun.

Your father worked nights as a parking lot attendant to make money to pay for his graduate school education. While more privileged students were musing about how to find work that spoke to their souls, your dad showed up for work without fail. He wasn't particularly interested in parking lot management, but he was dedicated to doing the best job that he could do.

After a year of consistent results, he was promoted to a day job in management. A decade and several career moves later, he now manages operations at a major airport and has discovered an intense love for the aviation industry. His major lesson learned is that rather than making a search for passion the cornerstone of his career development, passion evolved as a side effect of developing expert knowledge and demonstrating leadership.

Your mother has invested 15 years in attaining education and professional experience in the study of human behavior. She now specializes in helping individuals and organizations with workplace challenges. Almost weekly, she receives phone calls and emails from people who would like to interview her about the work she does. Many of the calls end with the interviewer mentioning that he or she would like to do similar work, only it would be nicer to skip all those years of graduate school and professional-dues-paying in diverse work settings.

Alec, honey, there are no short cuts!

Enjoy the journey along the way to success because that is where the best learning takes place. Trust that it feels good to look back over a solid track record of accomplishments. Believe that exhibiting character and discipline yields more benefits than costs, even when the costs are all that you can see in the short term and the long term seems a bit far off.

And finally, please do not take work too seriously. Work is but one sphere in a rich, full existence. Now that we have had you in our lives for 14 enchanting months, we wish we had made time for you earlier. As much as we value our jobs, there are no moments that are more fulfilling than the ones in which your sparkling eyes and baby smiles capture our attention.

If you inherited our ambition and drive and you find yourself planning out your future while still in high school, could you remember to make time to find your life partner and possibly make some grandchildren for us?

We love you, Alec, and we are sure you will have much to teach us.

Since writing this letter, **Michael and Janet** have been blessed with a second pregnancy and are eagerly awaiting the birth of their daughter, Carissa.

• • •

Dad Taught Me the Secret

Mark Servodidio

Work: Solves people-problems with a great sense of humor

Mark Servodidio is Executive Vice President of Human Resources for Cendant Car Rental Group (parent company of Avis and Budget Rent-a-Car). He's writing to his kids, ages 11 to 4.

DEAR NICHOLAS, BENJAMIN, EMILY, AND MICHAEL,

As I reflect on what lessons I have learned during my career that are worth passing on, so many come to mind. I could talk about the importance of spending more time at home and less time in the office, or treating people with dignity and respect, or following your dreams by doing what you love, or having courage to make the right decisions. All of these are worth reflecting on, and are important.

But for me, there is one thing that embodies all of these, as well as ensuring your happiness and success. For me, the secret behind everything is your work ethic — your attitudes, beliefs, and determination to stay focused on what is important to you.

I learned this secret from your grandfather. For years, every Saturday, without fail, he'd come in and wake my brothers and me out of bed. Every Saturday morning began with "Nighttime is for sleeping, daytime is for working. It's daytime, so let's go…"

We would then proceed to do every imaginable chore around the house — usually until dusk — then enjoy a great meal, and head off to bed. I know what you're thinking: This does not sound like a fun way to spend half a weekend! But in many respects, those days are among my fondest memories of growing up.

During those days, I would learn many practical skills while being able to listen to and learn from my father. The work built strong relationships with teammates (brothers relying on each other for help — developing a give-and-take); gave me the stamina to do what it takes (don't quit until the job is completed); provided a safe environment to make mistakes without fear of reprisal (usually!); taught me about faith and vision (being connected, and working toward a greater cause and purpose than just the task at hand); as well as teaching me about trust, respect, communication, difficult decisions, laughing, patience…all things you need to know to be both happy and successful.

What I struggle with is how to pass these things on to you. You probably wouldn't tolerate such Saturday rituals, and I don't know if I'd want to put you through them anyway.

There's so much to pass on to you…

But I feel confident we've given you a good start down the right path. We'll discover the rest together.

All my love, Dad

Mark Servodidio's day job — dealing with mergers, cost-cutting, and operations snafus — often makes him feel like the "bad guy." That's why he's also on the board of a nonprofit organization serving preschoolers. He likes being the "good guy."

• • •

Be Contagious!

Dave Woods

Work: Helps and inspires others to learn and take personal risks

Dave Woods is now an independent productivity maven. This comes only after he's tried, many times, to be a loyal corporate employee, and failed every time. He is writing to his kids, Meg, age 15, Greg, 13, and Brennan, 11. Dave is supported and encouraged by his partner in life, Pam.

DEAR MEG, GREG, AND BRENNAN,

To be blunt, my career has been less than enriching. I'd like to get the *downs* out of the way, only so I can then dwell on the *ups*.

I have come up short in the neverending quest for a meaningful role at work. From big companies, to midsized companies, to start-ups, I simply have not found my stride. I have become tired of the constant push for productivity, sales, headcount reductions, and the like.

During many quarterly cycles in my past, I have worked on ways to cut costs, ways to ship product sooner, or ways to meet other stretch goals. Even though I was supposed to improve business results, I felt like the Scoreboard Guy at a baseball game — who posts the results every inning, and shouts for a better score, but has no ability to impact the on-field talent, the team morale, or the quality of the head coach.

To be clear, I do love business. But I think the business process needs to start with people. With financials simply being the end-result of focused people, and stretch goals being accomplished via an engaged workforce. I don't see that today.

But I do see subtle change; people are slowly leading the revolution to a people-centered work environment. In part, we can thank the demographic shifts in the U.S., which are slowly creating more demand for all-aged workers.

I have taken career risks for the sake of our family — reducing travel time and increasing family time, all while making money to pay the bills. This has been a tough balance, and it has always seemed like I had to choose one or the other.

That is why this is a story of bad news and good

news; I chose the family and my personal passions every time. In the process, I am constantly asked what I do for a living, since I am the Dad, and need to gently explain my transitions. It's hard; a man's stability is many times measured by his tenure on the job.

For me, the question has been *Why?* Why have I not found my stride, a fulfilling career?

My preferences are to put people and their needs first; and every corporate culture I encountered put company needs first. The corporate cultures had job descriptions and standard processes, and I longed for creativity in how I achieved those goals. No wonder my "successes" were always on the home front.

Our family is the center of everything. I can honestly say I have been there for you. Been there for the music lessons, been there to coach baseball, been there to do family outreach and establish family traditions, been there to see every concert and every play, been there to provide support when you have fallen down or needed guidance, and been there to celebrate every possible excuse for a family occasion.

Because of my quest for self-realization, and because of my many failings, I can help you profile yourself to better understand your preferences and career options. Second, I can help you learn from my failings, in as much detail as you'd like. And third, I can help teach flexibility. While one's moral fiber must always stay intact, flexibility in marriage, careers, friendships, and adversity is a necessity.

I can help teach you to problem-solve. The adversity of losing my mother at a young age,

the adversity of not finding meaningful work,
and the adversity of taking a nontraditional path
have all made me a creative problem-solver. Life will
have plenty of adversity, and you can learn from my
mistakes to lessen your first-hand pain, and develop
your personal toolkit for life. In fact, since you are
such great kids, it's the least I can do.

In my corporate years, I was taught conforming
things: Conform to policies, conform to measurements
and standard processes, conform to dress codes, etc.
In reality, people need to express themselves.

When I recognize the reality that I will be
working full- or part-time until I am near age 80,
health permitting, I am excited about doing the kind
of work I am passionate about — helping others.
Along the way, I have surprised myself with all that I
have learned from you, my kids. I have learned not to
"major in minors," I have learned to be more flexible
in how and when work (housework!) actually gets
done, and I have learned how to influence and
motivate others, instead of simply direct them.
All from my kids. These skills were learned not as
a corporate man, but as a family man.

I am now contagious! Everything I have taught
you, my kids, I have now learned myself. I am ready
to positively affect the lives of others, and help them
on their journey.

Thanks kids; I promise to keep it simple, treat
others fairly, be selfless, and make a difference.

Dave Woods also teaches, coaches baseball, and leads several outreach
programs to support the homeless and disadvantaged.

Leave an Enduring Legacy

Dave Ulrich

Work: Helping leaders lead from their heart, as well as their bottom line

Dave Ulrich is on leave as Professor of Business at the University of Michigan to serve with his wife as mission president for the Montreal, Canada Mission of the Church of Jesus Christ of Latter-day Saints. They chase, help, inspire, serve, and teach 200 19-25-year-old missionaries for three years. It keeps them young, but makes them feel old.

DEAR GREAT-GREAT-GRANDFATHER JAMES LEITHEAD,

In 1832, at age 16, you left Scotland to live with your uncle in Nova Scotia. You lived between Montreal and Toronto where, in 1836, you met a young man named Parley Pratt, converted to his faith, then subsequently moved to Nauvoo, Illinois, then Utah. The decisions you made in your life affect our lives 175 years later.

This letter is my chance to return and report to you how I have upheld the legacy you began.

Today, my wife Wendy and I lead the missionary efforts in Quebec and Ottawa for the church you joined so long ago. In doing this work, we have drawn on lessons learned from 20 years of writing, teaching, and consulting.

Focus on what matters most. We cannot be all things to all people. Organizations, leaders, and missionaries need to learn what matters most, then dedicate resources of time, energy, and passion to accomplish those things. We must define for ourselves what matters, not let someone else do it for us. Most of what matters comes from our deepest values, and folds a long-term vision into short-term actions.

Wendy and I have learned through this missionary assignment what matters most to us. When we were asked by church leaders to serve a three-year full-time mission, we were honored and surprised. It was both a hard and an easy decision. It was hard to walk away from a successful career and leave behind both financial success and professional acclaim. It was harder to consider being away from family and friends for three years. But it was easy because we have covenanted that we would consecrate our time and talents to serving God and others, and we see this assignment as a means for doing so. Our decision to accept this calling was made in a day, but formed over generations. I can now begin to imagine how, 175 years ago, you found it both hard and easy to move because of your religious convictions.

Give back. There is both an obligation and opportunity for the privileged to give back. Giving back focuses attention on those who receive by figuring out what they want and need. Companies give back in ways that add value to employees, customers, and shareholders; people give back in service that provides meaning to others. The best leaders I know give back through both private and public charities.

We have been enormously blessed financially and professionally. Wendy and I have always looked for ways to give back through our family (time with kids and parents), profession (editing journals and being responsive to colleagues), and church service (this and other assignments). We find that giving back is one of those things that is difficult to schedule and do at times, but after we have done it, we feel better about ourselves.

This assignment is seven days a week, twenty-four hours a day. We are on call to serve the missionaries we supervise. I am learning — begrudgingly at times — that to give back means to give up some sense of autonomy and control of my time and energy. When I am in the middle of writing or thinking about something, I inevitably get a phone call which, in my old world, would have been a distraction, but in this world is my *raison d'être*.

Find peace from the inside/out. Our present world is filled with conflicts between nations, competition between companies, and challenges in relationships. We cannot control the world, but we can control our reaction to it. To find enduring peace in the midst of contention, we should focus on what we do more than what we do not do; build on, and leverage our strengths; and constantly improve by learning both from what works and what does not. Through regular self-assessment, we define and develop an inner source of peace that gives us confidence in uncertain futures.

In taking our current assignment, we have come to peace with clients and ourselves. Almost all of our friends and clients expressed enormous support, captured by one saying: "In the war for talent, God wins." Coming to peace with ourselves meant redefining our scorecard of success. Making money, writing articles and books, teaching classes, and impacting businesses were easy scorecards to monitor. Now, we measure success in less tangible ways as we try to influence about 500 missionaries who will serve with us over three years as we try to establish a church in this area.

We are constantly doing self-assessments to learn how to improve what we do, and while making mistakes along the way, we are getting better at doing it. For example, I have never been very gracious with service incompetence (e.g., in airlines, car rentals, restaurants, bureaucracy, etc.). In this present assignment, I wear a name badge with my name and the church I represent. So, when I become agitated, the person in front of me can simply look at my name badge and I feel shame for badly representing my church. I have not yet overcome my insolent tendencies, but I am working on them a little at a time.

Change small and simple things. As we try to improve, we are drawn to the large, dramatic, and splashy programs for change, but we are impacted more by the small and simple changes in our daily routines. We don't change the world through epiphanies, but by doing lots of little things that add up to sustained transformation. Simple things are not always easy to change, but by improving one thing at a time, we make progress toward great things.

Wendy and I seek daily little things that we can tweak to make our lives better. In this assignment, the simple things include grooming (1,000+ days in white shirt and tie and clean-shaven — a record for my lifetime!), reading (replace novels with scriptures), thinking and writing (more about topics like hope, faith, commitment, peace, and charity rather than market value, customer commitment, and strategic human resources), attention (spending time dealing with people more than organizations), and behavior (working to be sensitive to the needs of others and follow the principles we preach). While far from perfect, we are making personal progress to learn how to do this new assignment.

This is my report. The legacy you began endures. I hope that Carrie, Monika, and Michael will continue and build on the legacy you began and we have nurtured.

Until we meet, Dave

Dave Ulrich has written a dozen books on leadership and management, serves on the Board of Directors of Herman Miller Inc., and was ranked by *Business Week* magazine in 2001 as the Number One business educator.

• • •

Be a Respectful Rebel

Rick Ritacco

Work: Makes sense of 1's and 0's for people who have stuff to say

Rick Ritacco recently left Pitney Bowes Financial Services as a member of their executive staff. He's now CEO of a Web development firm. He's writing to his son and daughter, Ricky, age 16, and Alison, 12.

DEAR RICKY AND ALISON,

First and foremost, I have had the privilege to be married to one of the most giving, understanding, supportive, caring, and forgiving women on the face of the earth. I also am blessed with two children that a father cannot help being extremely proud of. This is lesson number one: **If you have a strong and supportive family with a true belief in God,** everything else is secondary. Marry your best friend, have children, and teach them to be responsible caring adults who give more to the world around them than they take. Really, I mean really live the old saying "Family comes first."

Sure everyone at the office always says, "Family come first," but these are the same people that I was working with until 9:00 every night. How does working 12- to 14-hour days put family first?

I learned this lesson the hard way. I accepted a position to launch a new product in Canada and commuted from Connecticut to Mississauga every week for five months. You two were nine and five. Every time I returned home you both had seemed to change. I lost five months of watching you both grow up, and that's time I can't get back.

My second lesson is to **never stop learning and complete your "formal" education** before you have so many responsibilities that interfere. I left school for a variety of reasons and had to deal with many challenges that having a young family can create when trying to balance family, work and school. Treat every class, every lesson as if it were the last bit of learning you would ever receive; learn everything you can, hunger for knowledge and don't blindly accept things that don't make sense; challenge the teacher if you don't agree.

I had to struggle to get my career going, lacking a formal degree. I had to work harder than others to show my worth. Now, one advantage of not having a formal degree is that I always considered myself the "dumbest" person on the teams that I formed or managed. This caused me to listen to everyone and not think I had all of the answers. We truly achieved great things because of a genuine team effort, not one person dictating to a bunch of Yes people.

This leads me to lesson number three: **Speak up if you don't agree, and take on any project/opportunity that comes your way. Be a rebel.** Corporations have too many Yes people for their own good. This is how companies lose their competitive edge.

Businesses are built by someone who creates a new product or service, or improves the way a product is made or a service is performed. These creators are not Yes people — they are rebels. Be a rebel, a respectful rebel, but a rebel nonetheless. If your employer doesn't like someone who shakes things up, go somewhere that respects that quality in an individual (this will be the successful company in the long run). There have been times when I disagreed with a decision and didn't speak up or didn't use my influence to change the decision. I now regret my cowardice.

I have learned from those regrets and have since stood alone in front of critics while the rest of my teammates (who held the same belief as I) abandoned our cause like rats off a sinking ship. Stand your ground and hold true to your beliefs. They can only fire you, they can't beat you!

I have never failed. Now, that's a big statement. I have failed to succeed, but I have never failed or quit. Only quitters fail. Give everything you set out to do 100%.

Be modest and don't worry about getting the credit for a job well done; you will never get as much credit as you deserve. Be happy within yourself knowing that you did a kick-ass job.

And remember, don't dwell on your failures or rest on your successes; get on with your next adventure, because time's-a-wastin'.

Lesson four: **Have fun and laugh every day.** Remember to have fun at home, at work, and at play. Having fun will make you a happier person and you will be a better family member, do a better job and live longer. If you are not having fun at work, find something that is fun for you.

Countless numbers of coworkers have told me that I had the best job in the company (I have held nine different positions and have heard this through all of them). Why is this? Because I enjoyed every position I held and made it mine. I made it something I loved to do. The coworkers saw my smiling face, my laughs, and my positive attitude. They didn't see me working until three in the morning to make a deadline, or pulling a week of all-nighters. They saw someone who loved what he did.

In the office, and outside the office, surround yourself with happy people. You will meet many people in your life; learn from them, laugh with them, help them and cherish the time you spend with them. If they are not uplifting, help them be uplifted.

If they can't be uplifted, find people who are.

Don't waste time on tears. Instead find a reason to laugh.

Remember we are only on this earth for a short time. Make the earth turn, don't just sit and watch it. Have a positive impact.

I will always be proud of you.

Your loving father,
Dad

Rick Ritacco sits on several nonprofit boards, and enjoys life in Connecticut with his wife of 20 years. His biggest problem is how to improve his golf game while maintaining a high handicap. He is looking forward to his dream career — a mix of being Santa Claus, Jimmy Buffett, and Tiger Woods combined.

DISCOVERY

FINDING THE CHOICES THAT
REALLY MATTER

"Time is what our people give to the company but
never get back."

• • •

"The fact that I can choose how hard and where to work
is a blessing."

• • •

"I have not always chosen wisely.

I must now reap what I had sown."

• • •

"Were you there? Did you do that? Did you speak up?
Was it wrong? Yes or No?"

You are defined by your choices.

Every day you make hundreds of tiny choices...

Which things to do, people to see,
meetings to attend, emails or calls
to answer — all based on a mixture
of fear, vision, passion, pride, joy,
loyalty, material needs, love,
and friendship.
Only a precious few of these choices
will lead you to what really matters.

• • •

Q: Do you know what's the number one
behavior in business today?
A: Passing to-do's onto someone else's plate.[†]
(Really!)

• • •

So what?
You should be questioning a lot more
of what you are asked to do.
Many of those requests are
other people's priorities, not yours.

• • •

Choose wisely.
There are only 1440 minutes in every day.
No do-overs.
Every choice takes you closer to
what's important to you, or steals
precious time from what you really
want to do, who you want to be with,
and how you want to be remembered.

• • •

Be aware. Get clear.
Know and claim the choices that lead you to —
or away from — what truly matters.

[†] see Endnotes & Stats, page 220

Choose to Do
What Is Right, Always

Rob Newson

Work: Keeping us safe

Rob Newson is a single father and a Commander in the U.S. Navy SEALS.
After 9/11, he was redeployed to various missions from his post as XO
(Executive Officer) of Special Boat Unit 12 and Navy SEAL Team Seven.
He continually writes to his three children, Aubrey, 15 years old, Chelsea, 13,
and Craig, 12, from wherever he is stationed in the world.

**AUBREY, CHELSEA, AND CRAIG –
MY BEST FRIENDS AND YOUNG CHARGES,**

As always, I miss your physical presence in my life
as the call to duty and country has separated us yet
again. When I am with you, I am whole. When I am
away, part of me is left behind.

So why do I do it? Why do I serve and sacrifice
and force your involuntary sacrifice as well? Simply,
it is the right thing to do. I am called to serve as
warrior and leader.

We live in both a wonderful and a horrible
world. We each choose, every day, which part of the
world we are from. To do wrong for a good cause is
still wrong.

Those Americans in Iraq in those horrible prison
pictures compromised themselves, hurt America, and
undermined all that we are fighting for. They are just
normal people who made very bad decisions.

We will all pay for their bad decisions with a

longer, harder war.

Some are good people who were caught up in doing evil. All should have said, "I am not doing this!"

The point is — you know what is right. Sometimes right is hard and wrong is easy. Do right anyway. Even if your boss or your friends, your boyfriend or girlfriend, or even me tells you to do wrong — it's your choice; choose wisely. No one can make you do wrong, no one can make a wrong right.

Most times it is not hard to tell wrong from right. The prison abuse in Iraq is not fuzzy or complex. Sometimes it is very hard to separate wrong from right and even harder to separate very wrong from not exactly right. War puts us in that position.

Outside of war — in your normal lives and chosen careers — many of your choices will not be black and white, but it is still important to separate right from wrong and always choose to do the right thing.

The lessons from war carry over into your everyday lives:

- **We cannot fight evil with evil** (or one set of wrongs with our own inappropriate choices and behaviors).
- **Right is right and wrong is wrong.**
- **Relativism is a lie:** Wrong cannot be justified.
- **Never compromise your values.**
- **Hold yourself accountable** for your actions AND your inactions: Silence in the presence of wrong-doing is complicity.
- **We all make mistakes,** we all chose badly at one

time or another — don't make excuses,
make corrections.

- **It's never too late to do the right thing.**

How can I teach these lessons to you, outside of war?
By living them, by talking to you about right and
wrong and by using real-life examples. Terrorism,
scandal, and inhumanity carry lessons both good and
bad that must be examined or they will be repeated.

Life's difficulty arises when faced with choosing
between the lesser of two evils, between unjust
sacrifice and illegitimate action. War places us all on
the razor's edge — protect by destroying, destroy by
protecting, or maintain a painful balance. There are
no easy choices but it is wrong to choose without
thinking, without weighing the costs.

Faced with right or wrong, everyone must
choose alone:

- Were you there?
- Did you do that?
- Did you speak up?
- Was it wrong?
- YES or NO?

It's about I and MY: "I did this; my decision was…"
It's not about They, We, or Them. Responsibility and
accountability for your decisions and actions cannot
be passed on to others.

I chose to follow the advice of columnist Thomas
Friedman and to teach you the same: "Repair that
jagged hole in the wall of civilization [created by 9/11]
by insisting, more firmly and loudly than ever, on
rules and norms — both for ourselves and for others."

In the end, we both live, and fight, by our

values...or we have no values. Choose wisely, my children.

I don't expect you to be perfect; no one is. What I ask is that you examine and understand the consequences of your actions and accept responsibility for your decisions. God put you in charge of your life, make Him proud.

I love you and I am very proud of you all.

After you read this, each of you write at least a paragraph in response: How do you make hard decisions? What values and ideals are important? Think on these things and decisions get easier!

Love, Dad

Rob Newson was one of 19 officers selected for a very special project at the turn of the new millennium — to envision the U.S. Navy of 2020, including how its leaders must lead. He is at the forefront of leadership development, bringing with him frontline, bottom-up experience. "In the SEALS, leaders go through everything with their team. There is no separate course for officers. You do everything they do, except you get yelled at more. The leader is part of the group. He's never above the fray. I think this is very important. Tomorrow's talent will not settle for anything less than leaders who address the challenges people face on the front lines."

• • •

Choosing Is a Privilege

Scarlett Hu

Work: Helps people use technology to learn, understand, and create

Scarlett Hu grew up in a small town in southern Taiwan. Her father worked with the U.S. Air Force and her family received old books from U.S. public libraries. From those books she learned English and a value system that led her to study and settle down in Los Angeles. She's currently an IT manager for the Getty Trust. She's writing to her 12-year-old daughter, Candace.

DEAR CANDACE,

The other day we fought over your obsession with an animation series, where the hero defeats his opponents with game cards with hidden magical power. You insisted that it is a passion, not an addiction, and that you know the difference between it and real life. You further said that you are tired of all the discipline we have been imposing on you.

You said you do not want to grow up to be like me or your father. You want to be happy.

By the way we live, Mommy and Daddy have sent you many messages about our values — frequently working late, and, in Daddy's case, working Saturdays and Sundays. Clearly, we are telling you that work is important and work is a major part of our lives. Clearly, we are telling you that one needs to work hard and be very dedicated. Our behaviors are probably more powerful messages than anything we could say.

As first-generation immigrants, Mommy and Daddy came from places where wars were never far away, and there were never enough essentials to go around. Indoctrinated to live with a sense of crisis, we worry, we conserve, and we compete. We don't seem to relax or enjoy life much.

But you, my dear, were born in this beautiful new world, where your father and I strived and finally arrived. Growing up in this country of freedom, hope, prosperity, and abundance, you are happy, generous, and dare to dream. So our messages of discipline seem to burden you.

You see, Mommy grew up with ranking and competition as daily topics in school. If there were 59 kids in my class (yes, class sizes were very large), one of us would have the number 59 written on the report card. That would hurt, and caused intense pressure at home to grow and improve.

I feel that you often seem to be afraid of competition and want to avoid it, except in the pretend-world of video games and animation. Maybe that's because victory for the hero is always assured. The consequences of defeat? Well, there is always the reset button. These games and animation almost seem like a sanctuary for you.

Whenever you have tried some of real life's competitions, you seem just as burdened by the possibility that you might lose as motivated by the potential to win. This is a natural feeling. At work or in life, the moments that stress me the most are always the moments that I feel or fear that I am left behind.

Competition, conservation, and other values from the old world, like creativity, freedom, humor, and fun-making, are all different facets of the prism of life. Except in real life, there is no magic that can be released from any spell, or pretend-weapon that mysteriously enhances your power and your chances of winning. Defeat is, sometimes, an inevitable outcome.

It's important for you to hear about defeats as

our society talks way more about victories.

Sometimes, you just don't get a fair chance to compete — like when I had to withdraw my application from a graduate school because I didn't have enough money. You can usually shrug off those kinds of disappointments with a "not fair!" and move on.

But sometimes you truly will have done your best, and it just won't be good enough. Remember one day when you were six, I came home from a job interview and I didn't want to talk, and you kept asking what was wrong? On that day, a company that I really wanted to join turned me down with almost insulting honesty — they told me how unsuitable I was for that job and their company. This kind of defeat, no doubt, is the hardest to accept and to reconcile within yourself. It took me months, if not longer, to recover. To this day, there is a scar somewhere in my memory.

Please remember that the ability to take defeat, to let go and restart, is ultimately the angel that will see you home.

Sometimes you will win, sometimes you will lose, and other times you will simply show up and be part of the experience. The showing-up part is very important. Why? Because you want to stay in the game so you can keep learning from it. Life can be more interesting than some of the most egregiously fantasized animations, with more fulfilling surprises.

Last week I learned that the company that I was dying to get into had hit hard times, and was laying off many of its employees. I would have been one of those now getting laid off. But, when I took their advice and sought opportunities in organizations very different from theirs, I joined a league that was more suitable for me. I survived, and learned a great lesson from it. To me, the greatest accomplishment in life is not to defeat or suppress your opponents but to prevail in an environment or under a system that may be holding you back or even oppressive to you.

Remember you asked me why I vote on everything? I said it's because my citizenship came by choice. I consider one of the greatest accomplishments in my life was to have the opportunity to choose my citizenship, and when I chose America, She chose me. For that, I am forever happy and content because there hasn't been a day in my life since that I haven't enjoyed the benefit of my choice.

This may seem strange to you. How can I be happy when I have to work so hard to stay that way? To me, the fact that I can choose how hard and where to work is a great blessing.

I remember my very best friend in fourth grade disappeared overnight because her parents put her to work in the family-owned nightclub. Her departure was so sudden, we didn't have a chance to say goodbye, and I never saw her again. She loved school, and would have done really well there and in her own career, if given the opportunity. Thinking about her, and what she lost, and what I now have makes me feel lucky and happy.

To see you believing that your right to make any choice (to not be like your parents, for example) is a birthright, is something that will always bring a smile to my face.

When I was about your age, I came across a poem that says that children's souls will go to places their parents can't even imagine. I know yours will, and I know you will find your happiness.

Whether you choose to be like me or not, my dear, I will always be here for you and ready to give you the best of my love.

Mommy,
At 6:30 P.M. in the office

Scarlett Hu's most precious memory of Candace was the day she returned after spending four months with her grandparents in Taipei. "That day, I felt like I had forced several years of growing up on my four-and-a-half year-old."

• • •

Choose Your Children's Childhood Over Work

Mary Anne Kochut

Work: Figuring out how to pay the bills, and enjoying being a grandma

Mary Anne Kochut has struggled to find work in her field, and five days after her savings ran out, took a temp job for one-third of what she used to make. Yet she's thankful they keep renewing her contract.

**TO NEW MOMS TRYING TO DECIDE
WHETHER OR NOT TO GO BACK TO WORK,**

I was waiting for the results of my biopsy. It was a

little after nine o'clock on the morning of September 11, 2001. My daughter called me and told me to turn on the television, and I went into shock with the rest of the world. I used to work in that neighborhood.

Here I am, unemployed, broke, waiting to hear whether or not I have cancer, and I want to do something. I'm not far from where the towers stood, but what could I do? I knew I couldn't stay home by myself. I went to church.

When I got back home, I checked my phone messages and there were none. However, when I checked the Caller-ID, I noticed that the doctor's office had called. I put two and two together and realized that if the results of the biopsy were benign, the doctor would have left a message. Since there was no message, the results were not good. At that point I knew that I had breast cancer.

I had surgery on October 1, and while I was in the hospital I had no visitors. (Both my daughters were unable to travel — one wasn't even well herself.) So, I was by myself.

I thought about all the times I contributed to gifts and signed cards for coworkers who were sick, and in the hospital. I remember contributing to help a coworker who was having financial problems after being disabled with breast cancer.

All my teammates were nowhere to be found now that I was no longer a part of that organization. Because I didn't have a job, there were no cards, flowers, or visitors.

This letter is not about regrets — it is about choices I've made, that maybe you'll have to make,

and then living with the results of those choices.
I have found that most people DO care, and want to
reach out to help. However, when choosing between
my children and my career, I have not always chosen
wisely. And I must now reap what I had sown.

My career was the most important thing to me.
I left my children with babysitters, as there weren't
the kind of day care services available then as there
are today. I hardly remember anything about their
childhood other than rushing them out of bed in the
morning, rushing to the babysitter, rushing to work,
picking them up at the end of the day, and then
rushing them into bed, and repeating the process
the next day.

When they were sick, I couldn't take off from
work to stay home with them, so they were bundled
up and went to the sitter. I was always busy, never
had time for them. I rushed them to grow up and
be independent.

After working for more than 20 years with
a large corporation, I took a voluntary retirement
package. By this time I was divorced, with one
daughter in college and the other one getting married.
All of the things I had put before them in the past
were now gone, and I didn't know what to do
with myself.

I began to realize how much of my self-image
was associated either with my job or my marital
status. Logically, I knew there was more to me than
that, but emotionally, with those things gone, I felt as
if I had no value to offer anyone.

Being broke at the same time made everything

seem worse. I had more bills than I could pay.

My church and community provided strength, support, and hope. Someone would come up to me at church to shake my hand, and put a $50 or $100 bill in it. Sometimes I would get cards from people with money in them. I have health insurance and a prescription plan; however, there were the co-payments that I had to make and they were adding up. Lasting help came from a breast cancer organization — the Susan G. Komen Foundation — for which I'm eternally grateful.

With more financial security, I wanted to be productive again. As quickly as possible. I did volunteer work at a state agency where I could help people who were like me — unemployed and in need of support. Based on my corporate experience, I facilitated workshops on career management and communications for people who had recently lost their jobs. It's a very rewarding experience to be able to help others! It's good for me to be in front of people and presenting again. It keeps my skills current.

All of this is what I must sow. Life is about priorities, and I had my priorities mixed up.

Having a career and the money to purchase "things" for my daughters caused me to miss what was really important — just being there for them, being a mommy. It used to break my heart when my daughter would cry and cling to me when I left her with the babysitter. But I just ignored my feelings, and left her.

Now, the house is gone. The job is gone.

The money is gone. The marriage is over (thank God!). And I see life and priorities very differently. Money is important — you have to pay the bills and eat. However, money and material things are not more important than relationships — especially relationships with our children.

The irony of my choices is not lost on me. Now that I have lots of time, my daughters' schedules and "things" mean they're often too busy for me. I realize this is what I taught them, and that they learned it well.

Today, I have a sense of peace and a relationship with God that comes from within. I never had anything like this before, and my most important needs are met. However, I can't help but wonder what might have been different if I had not been too busy with my career to be a full-time mother.

I truly believe that discovering that I had breast cancer on September 11th, 2001, was no coincidence. It put things into perspective.

The people who went to work and died on that fateful day thought they would be going home at the end of the day. They didn't, and I'm still here. I completed treatments in July of 2002. I am cancer-free. All my test results have come back normal at each subsequent doctor's visit.

When you decide whether or not to go back to work, here is my suggestion: Embrace and enjoy the pleasures of motherhood.

Don't let anything get in the way of the most important part of your life — your children's childhood. People tried to tell me this, and I didn't listen. There is unbelievable fulfillment in being a mother. You can't put a price tag on it.

Mary Anne Kochut loves being a grandma to Jessica, 16 months old, and Brianna, 7 months old. And with all her unemployment, she's had lots of time for her children's adulthood, enjoying every moment she shares with Vicki, 33, and Lori, 29. She's been cancer-free for over two years. Mary Anne remains very active in church activities including her choir work for the Catholic Music Ministry, Refuge. "I truly believe that God is and has been leading me through this journey. Any success I might have is His, not mine."

• • •

Inner Voices
Journey Notes from the Gut

Choose to Put People First: No Exceptions

I was up all night with a knot in my stomach the size of a Volkswagen. Of course the manager under me should take the time to visit his sick mother. But if something goes wrong while he's gone, our CEO was looking for a reason to fire him. On the other hand, what if something happened to his mom? Would he ever forgive me? Would I ever forgive myself?

I sat in my office thinking how much I hated this horrible job. I always wanted a big job, but this was not at all what I thought it would be like. When I was a kid, I thought that when I was as old as my parents, I'd know what to do. I'd be different. Right.

After I laid out the situation for him, he decided to stay. Thankfully, his mother got better. But I never ever felt right about feeling I had to ask someone to make that kind of choice. It made me ashamed. I'd let the noise of my own job drown out what my heart knew to be true: People first, job second. No exceptions.

So, someday when you are at your job, if you find yourself in a bind between people and all the work that needs to get done, be smart and trust your heart to tell you what you know is right. Then follow it. It is the best and the only thing to do.

Our lives are like a picture hanging on the wall. Work is merely the frame for all the wonderful things that make up the photo of your life.

— That job and that decision are what caused **Lisa Dennis** to establish her own firm — "Someplace true," she says, "where people come first, and I can always make the right choice without feeling like I am jumping off a cliff." She runs the Boston Chapter of *Fast Company* magazine's Company of Friends network.

• • •

Choose to Believe: In Yourself, In Possibilities

Joan Malin

Work: Helps teenagers make informed choices and live with hope

Joan Malin is currently the CEO of Planned Parenthood of New York City.

TO ALL OUR TEENS, ESPECIALLY THOSE I SERVE,

I am lucky. I have always known on some level what I wanted to do and that work was important to me — that my life was going to be given meaning by the work that I would do.

Maybe this is because I grew up in an era of possibility, when social change was in the air, and I could help shape the world. It is also because I was raised by an enormously talented woman, who, as a single mom, held a full-time job, went to college at night, was a civil rights activist, and still found time to teach art classes to kids who were abandoned and living in the public hospital in Philadelphia. She believed in possibilities, and that we are all connected in very powerful ways.

This desire to be of use and to feel connected to the world, to develop a stronger sense of community in this society led me to become a city planner. What better goal than to literally build communities? I also liked planners; the tools they use — design, economics and history, and the way they think — analytic, yet people-oriented.

Growing up, I never knew that there was such a profession. Discoveries liked this helped me understand something very important: Consider the actual tasks involved in the work you would do every day. And follow those tasks into different fields. Which means never getting fixated on making one right career decision.

Your life may be about making that decision again and again, as I have done, and I have never regretted making changes.

I have gone from planning, to management, to advocacy, and from working on issues related to urban development to social services to women's reproductive health. I found that the skills and the passion are transferable. But the guiding principle is doing work that makes a difference, and that you can see and feel the impact of your work.

The second guiding principle: Working with good people, people with heart and brains. Following a belief in the possibilities of people and taking risks does lead to meeting and working with extraordinary people. The combination of both makes you want to go to work every day. That feeling is essential and when it is not there, for me, it is time to move on.

I once took a position in state government, developing low-income housing. I took the job because I was exhausted from my position, working for an elected official. It was a real high-wire act, lots of pressure and yet ultimately not satisfying. I could not see the impact we made. The fit wasn't right.

I am now the CEO of Planned Parenthood of New York City. For me, our work of providing health care services and educational programs and advocating for the needs of women and families directly connects to my work in planning, and building community. We help people to take care of themselves, and when they cannot, we seek to insure that there is a safety net for them. Every day, I get to see the positive effect of our work in young people's lives and that makes it all worthwhile. And I work with extraordinary, talented, smart, compassionate people.

The next important principle to follow, I learned later in life, and that is not to take yourself seriously. The work that you do must matter, but others can do what you do, and maybe better. Let go, and just love the work. And give others the opportunity to do the same.

Finally, our lives are fragile — the sum of our experiences, relationships, desires, and priorities are what matters to us. The world is different if only knowing you expands one person's life. We are fed by these relationships, by this love, and we give it in return. And if we do nothing else, our lives will have mattered.

Joan Malin's many years of working inside its government forged a love of New York City, which continues to grow stronger every day. She strives always to make real the connections between her work and her life, and to live with passion.

...

Choose Love Over All Else

Linda Chezem

Work: Making a difference to future generations

Linda Chezem is a professor at Purdue University School of Agriculture as well as a part-time professor at the Indiana University School of Medicine. She wrote this letter to her son, on the eve of his taking his legal bar exam, and to her daughter who was entering college, to explain why she chose to resign from the Indiana Court of Appeals. "The simple answers do not satisfy most lawyers who want what I had," she says. "I have not regretted the decision even when I am not sure what to do next. But putting my explanation on paper is very intimidating as years of training in legal writing taught me to exclude myself from the facts of the case."

DEAR ANDY AND SALLY,

It is difficult for me not to rush in with advice and other misguided attempts to smooth your path. I have been given my life and my tasks, and you have yours. All I can do for you is to love you and hold you in my prayers each day and that I do.

Why didn't I stay on the Court or why didn't I practice law and make money or attain prestige? The answer lies in my belief that I can now work in ways of importance to your generation and those that follow. I am grateful for the opportunity to work with Dean Victor Lechentenberg and Dr. T.K. Li. Their intelligent and caring approach to building learning institutions for the generations that are coming is an inspiration to all who love young people. They have each given a legacy, one to Purdue, and the other to Indiana University, that will last several generations.

I did not leave so much as I was seeking to find better ways to work with others.

Many of the answers you seek for my leaving the Court can be found through reading. I commend to you this list: *Servant Leadership* by Robert Greenleaf and *Love and Profit* by James Autry are my picks of modern literature about how we go about work. For the poetry in your life, I recommend the Psalms, Robert Blake, Shakespeare, Emily Dickinson, and Robert Frost. When life gets to feeling like drudgery and dreariness, poets have the ability to lift the clouds and let you see distant goals more clearly.

I left the reading of the Bible to the end of this list, and in its own paragraph, because of its importance and some dangers in reading it. I hope that you will read the Bible and find it to be a guide to your relationship with God. My belief in God's unconditional love for all mankind has been pivotal in my life and the Bible has guided me to that faith.

But I have also seen faith and the Bible misused by those who would lay down rigid rules on belief and behavior in proof of their own righteousness. I have fled their churches and their words with horror at their omission of the very thing God was trying to teach his children through the Bible and with Jesus — his love for you and me.

It seems so simple that we should take the words of God into our hearts and make ourselves reflections of his love.

I hope that your life's work will be good for you and not just a means to accumulate material stuff. I want you to make enough money that you can do well by yourself and others. I wish that you can have money to give in love to others. I do not want to see great neon domes named after your gifts but I hope to hear the stories of quiet help that let a family get on its feet or a student finish school. Helping someone you do not know in a crucial and quiet way is the mark of a loving person. Helping without seeking thanks is a gift to the giver. The most dangerous kind of giving is trying to control through gifts. That is not giving; that is buying someone's will in a cruel way. God has made clear that love is the wanted gift and the only one you can take with you.

So wherever you go, whatever your work becomes, love well, often, and intensely, and success will follow.

Linda Chezem was finally ready to write this letter and explain her choices after

"wandering western Montana and northern Idaho, and soaking up the peace."
She also reflected on, and reread a collection of letters from her great-great-
great-grandfather before he died of battle wounds in the Civil War. "What his
letters meant to me is a part of what I would write to my children," she shared.

• • •

Inner Voices
Journey Notes from the Gut

Time Matters: Choose Wisely
It was only recently that I really learned the true face
of time. It happened when I began to look seriously
at quality of life. For me, the notion of work/life
balance has meant that I talk about it a lot, but rarely
practice it. I merely watch the second hand sweep,
and wonder where those precious moments went.

So I asked those lucky few I know who had
successfully balanced work and life, how they did it.
Their answers were all very similar, and had nothing
to do with stretching an extra hour into a day.
Instead, it was simpler. Many saw that it revolved
around cherishing and worshipping the time that they
had. As one executive said, "Time is what our people
give to the company but never get back." Or as
someone else pointed out, they exchange their lives
for however many weeks of holidays a year and
therefore every other moment of life has to be
cherished — when there is time.

These ideas came home to me when talking to a
former corporate high flyer about his recently
diagnosed leukemia that gave him only a short time
to live. He made it clear that time is really all we

have, some long and some very short, so make the best of every moment. While I can conceptualize this, I never really make it my mantra; I never quite manage to keep it at the forefront of my mind.

So to you, my son Christopher and daughter Amelia, who have many years before joining the crazy working world, I only hope that you will remember to make the best use of every moment when you do get there.

— **Julian Chapman** is a Lieutenant Colonel in the Canadian Army Reserve, and works nine-to-five as a business trainer in Toronto. While he champions effective thinking in the workplace, he'll be the first to admit that he inadvertently and too frequently does not practice what he preaches.

• • •

Always Choose Family

Lance Tracy

Work: Helps everyone inside and outside of companies play nice in the same sandbox

Lance Tracy specializes in performance engineering and implementing corporate outsourcing efforts. Prior to a recent round of layoffs, he was a director for a division of ADP, the benefits and payroll outsourcing firm.

DEAR BABY TRACY,

When I originally set out to write this letter, your mother was working near our home in California and I was out of the country leading an offshore outsourcing implementation. While I was away, your mother experienced complications with her pregnancy and we lost the child. I couldn't make it back for several days and, without any real support structure nearby, your mother endured the ordeal alone. By the time I made it home, it was over. I had missed taking her to the hospital, sitting with her in the waiting room, supporting her during the exams and tests...and being with her when the doctor told her the baby had miscarried.

It took a while for me to actually understand what had happened. I wrestled with how things might have been different if I had been closer to home, and questioned the priorities I had communicated when I was unable to return until days after your mother entered the hospital. I soon realized that while I couldn't change what had happened, I could resolve that it wouldn't happen again.

Fate being what it is, I was given a chance to honor this promise. Six weeks ago, I learned that you were on the way and two weeks later, an emergency had your mother back in the hospital. This time, I was working on a project on the other side of the country when she called...but luckily, it only took an hour (and some fancy work by the Ft. Lauderdale Delta Airlines desk) to get me on my way home.

I saw you for the first time a few days later. The ultrasound showed you as tiny, dark and grainy, but what we were looking for — a heartbeat — came through strong and clear. Despite the shadow of uncertainty from prior tests, you were doing just fine.

As I stood there, holding your mother's hand and staring at you on the screen, I realized, truly for the first time, that there were more important things than work. Up to that moment, I lived only for bigger projects, tougher assignments, and the chance to tackle more complex business problems.

Pursuit of greater challenges had truly blinded me to the importance of family, friends, and, to some degree, my own well-being.

You, in a sublime way, have revealed this to me...and I know I can only be better as a result. Thank you.

Since writing this letter, **Lance Tracy** and **Liezl dela Cruz-Tracy** became the proud parents of Samara Ravyn. While work is still important, family takes precedence. Lance and Liezl moved from California to South Carolina to be closer to Samara's grandparents and to provide Liezl with a better support network in case there are further medical issues. Lance has also accepted a position with Accenture, in part, because they'd allow him to office at home.

• • •

Choose What *You* Want

Alexis Harley

Work: Helps her company stay out of hot water

Alexis Harley is currently a Senior Analyst of Enterprise Risk Management. What's that, you wonder? She wishes she knew too....Alexis is a degreed chemical engineer and performed neurology research to support herself through college. She's writing to her five-year-old daughter Nikki.

DEAR NIKKI,

Sometimes, leaving my desk feels like pulling gum from the bottom of a shoe. The majority of my thoughts let go after a decisive, concentrated pull, but small filaments cling, only separating when distance (like the subway ride home) stretches them beyond their resistive capacity.

You see, Mommy *flexes* her time — that's a good '90s initiative worth capturing here for posterity. When I returned to work after maternity leave, I needed to work full time, but I couldn't stand the thought of having someone else (even though that someone was my own mother) provide your care for all of your waking hours five days a week. Although my company had various policies supporting alternative work schedules, I knew of no one who ever proposed the schedule I designed. The typical arrangement, judging by the two people I know personally, and the mass experience disclosed within parenting and working mother magazines, was to work from home a full day or two each week. This arrangement always has a clear end-date, with Mom going back to the way things were before pregnancy.

I, however, wanted to come into the office all five days, but leave at 3 P.M. with the understanding that, barring an urgent need, I would fulfill my remaining work obligation after you were put to bed for the night. I wanted this arrangement indefinitely.

In the beginning, when you woke up at 5 A.M., napped when I was at the office and stayed up until 10 P.M., I thought that the HR department had granted my wish because they secretly knew that I was doomed to failure on all fronts. I actually felt a kinship with prisoners of war, understanding why sleep deprivation is considered a form of torture.

I was unfocused both in the office and at home.

But over time, as your schedule evolved, I managed both motherhood and occupation increasingly better. I grew more accepting of my limitations. Although I am painfully aware that spreading my talents across multiple trades makes me a master of none, I have come to be content with maintaining equilibrium between my dependability as a parent and my employability as a professional.

So…where was I?

Oh yes, pulling gum from a shoe….

It is somewhere on the ride home from work that I make the mental transition from Risk Management Analyst to Mommy. Some days the transition is easy — I've reached a comfortable juncture in my To Do list and leave work non-conflicted. Other days, I'm stunned to realize that I actually long for more office time.

Then I consider the consequences.

If I stay later today, I may be tempted to do so next month, next week, or even as soon as tomorrow. There are lots of good reasons to make small exceptions today. Problem is, they tend to snowball. That's why I force myself to step back and view things from the broader context.

Do I really want to accelerate my work experience at the price of experiencing you less? Given that I have about 35 more years until I retire, will it really impact my long-term career potential if I veer onto the slow-track for a while?

My advice to you is to always stay keenly aware that your current options are indeed current, and only represent a fraction of your life possibilities.

Also remember that few choices are truly irreversible. Dorothy in *The Wizard of Oz* may have had to travel home by a completely different route than that by which she came; nevertheless she did return to where she truly wanted to be.

Love, Mommy

Alexis Harley is a single mom, and lives with her parents and Nikki in Brooklyn, New York. She remarks that single parenthood has created in her an amazing personal transformation: "Before, I was more hesitant to speak up for my needs, more conscious of the impact of certain decisions on my career path, more inclined to pursue new heights on the corporate ladder by traditional climbing techniques. Being a single working parent encumbered me in many ways, yet freed me in many others. I think acting on behalf of another in addition to yourself magnifies the significance of the justifications and consequently buttresses your resolve."

• • •

Choose to Love the Ropes

Bronwyn Fryer

Work: Helps others understand work, business, life

Bronwyn Fryer is a senior editor with the *Harvard Business Review* and an itinerant screenwriter. She is writing to her 12-year-old daughter, Morgan.

DEAR MORGAN,

I guess you could say I have a very cool job. I'm constantly meeting very interesting and amazing people.

But you know, I didn't always have cool jobs. I grew up pretty poor. Nobody helped me out financially.

So from the time I was 15 until after I was in graduate school, I held a lot of jobs that felt fairly unpleasant at the time — bussing tables and washing dirty dishes, cleaning out motel toilets, waiting tables on the graveyard shift at a pancake house, emptying ashtrays at a dance club, chopping up negatives at a 24-hour photo facility and, later on, grading mountains of badly written student papers. These didn't really require a lot of creativity or intelligence, but they paid the rent.

I want to tell you that you, too, will probably have some uncool jobs as you grow up. You may have work that will make you tired and grumpy, work that leaves you unchallenged, even depressed. Sometimes you'll have to work with people you don't like, even people who are mean.

If you work with someone who treats you rudely, it's an opportunity to remember your martial arts: Take the force coming at you and outwit it. (Remember, the psychological problems that cause people to be mean are theirs, not yours. You must learn to ignore and short-circuit their negativity.) This is not to say you should tolerate abuse — no one should. If a situation is intolerable, you must leave the job (preferably, not before you've found a better one to take its place).

On your way to where you want to go, try to see each job as a stepping stone from here to there. If you are brave, self-disciplined and take big steps, you will reach your goal faster.

As you step, think of each stone as part of a larger learning process. Even menial service jobs have something to teach. For example, waitressing taught me to multitask, a skill that has always come in handy.

I also learned to have great compassion for people who might not have the opportunity to get better jobs, as you will.

I really appreciate the efforts of the waitress who serves me coffee, the maid who cleans my hotel room, the guy who vacuums my car at the car wash. I try to let them know, by being kind, generous and friendly, that I've been where they are and that they are not invisible.

You will one day have a job — maybe even a series of jobs — that you truly love.

As you travel on that path, think about the next stone, and the next one, and the next one after that. You have always wanted to be an artist. To get there, you will need to work very hard, be very self-disciplined, and do some things that you don't like.

So if you find yourself scrubbing, flipping, changing diapers, or studying math, try to enjoy the moment and appreciate whatever you can, no matter how small — the smile of a customer, the laughter of your coworkers, the smell of the baby's skin, the scratch of the pencil. Try to keep the appreciation in your heart, and let the negativity go by deep breathing, as I have taught you. Try to see the big picture and remember that all work, even the most seemingly uncool kind, is special and important.

Remember my favorite Zen adage, the one about "loving the ropes"? Two people are tied up in chairs with ropes and chains. One person struggles to get free, and ends up bruised, bleeding, and frustrated — and stays just as tightly chained as ever. The other decides to love the ropes — and the ropes fall right off.

Sure, I still have to do a few unpleasant things on my cool job. But as I do them, I try to breathe deeply and appreciate how far I've come. I try to focus on enjoying being alive, and working (finally!) at a job I love and feel I was born to do.

My path has been longer and more painful than I suspect yours will be, but I'm glad to have arrived. And you will arrive, too, as long as you can remember to keep your eyes on the prize and your heart open.

If you learn, learn, learn with the mind of a beginner as long as you live, I promise you will have a cool journey.

I love you, my best bear.
Mom

One of **Bronwyn Fryer's** most wonderful memories of Morgan, which continues still, is watching her sleep. "When you watch your children sleep you see them revert to earlier phases of childhood and infancy. I love to smell her golden hair and her skin, and to see her mouth open in that gentle O. These moments produce a lovely ache for me: The sorrow of saying goodbye to her childhood, the fear of danger and the longing to protect her from the world, but most of all the appreciation for the great gift she is, and the gut-wrenching, pure love that is motherhood."

Choose to Live Out Loud, Every Day

Ellen Glassman

Work: Designing how people, products, joy, and profits all come together

Ellen Glassman is General Manager for Design and Strategy at Sony
Electronics, in Park Ridge, New Jersey. She wrote this work diary as
introspective therapy — a reminder about waking up to what really
matters — and hopes others can learn from her experience.

At 4:30 A.M., May 16, 2004, the phone awakens me.
My mother says "Something's wrong with Jennifer.
The baby's OK, but I want you to prepare yourself,
I don't think she's going to make it. The doctors say
they don't think she's going to survive. They think
you should come now."

I rush to pack a bag, chanting over and over,
pleading with God, "Don't take my Jen-Jen."

The ride from Closter, New Jersey, to Beth
Israel Hospital in Brookline, Mass., is a surreal
experience. Clasping my cell phone the entire time,
I keep thinking, *Phone, don't ring. If it rings, it's bad.
No ring means she's still alive.* My husband makes
an attempt at chit-chat about traffic on I-95. I am
floating in no-man's land making a contract with God
about how I'll repay Him for delivering a miracle.

Around 9:30 A.M. I rush into her ICU room. My
sister lies clinging to life. Her head seems three times
its normal size. Her eyelids have triple folds. Her ears
are misshapen. Her tongue hangs out of her mouth.

Her face is so swollen. My beautiful sister, I stroke her hair and repeat, "I love you my Jen-Jen."

Thirty years melt away as I imagine the childhood room we shared, twin faux Rococo beds, white and gilded on a sea of blue shag carpet. Now my sister's bloated body lay motionless on a white hospital bed. The hemorrhaging and swelling so severe they can't close her up, so they stuff her abdomen with towels, seal her belly with surgical Saran wrap, and drape a white sheet over her post-partum belly.

That most devastating day, I learn what really matters.

Now that I've returned to my harried life, my delicious children, my loving husband, my creative work, I often reflect on the six days I spent with my sister so that I can refocus my priorities. Likewise, I have found these "truths to be self-evident" in my long career at Sony:

Teamwork. Twenty-five doctors working at the top of their game under life and death pressure saved Jen.

Skill. Master-craftsman surgeons used their well-honed talent to piece Jen back together.

Resources. Jen's body took 21 units of blood — the entire hospital supply. And she needed special lung compression equipment from a neighboring hospital to save her life.

Commitment. Nurses, residents, and technicians worked tirelessly to normalize Jen's bodily functions.

Drive. My sister summoned her innermost strength to fight for her own life.

Relationships. The bonds built through our shared experiences are the most valuable "work-products" of our lives. My sister and I have never been closer.

Joy. Watching my sister hold her new baby for the first time after being in a coma for five days is a moment I'll never forget.

Faith. Above all else, it is essential to believe in what is possible, even against the odds.

These eight principles shape the way I conduct business at Sony, every day.

For example: Over 16 years I worked my way up Sony's organization, from a most junior designer to becoming Director of the East Coast Design Center. Recently, I transferred to Corporate Marketing as General Manager of Design and Strategy. Throughout that time, building positive relationships and teamwork with my new colleagues has been a top priority. Through email, phone calls, and meetings I seek insight on my fellow team members: What they care about and how they like to work. One of my team members has a brilliant sense of humor. My communication style with him is to sincerely applaud his cleverness and make an attempt at humor in kind. Another team member has impeccable project management skills and works at the speed of light. My style with her is one of hyper-promptness and short, bulleted executive summarizing of my next steps.

One of my first projects with my fellow marketing strategy officers was to develop our action plan for the coming year. Working together, we summarized the eight important projects our team would tackle along with the needed resources. Our one-page spreadsheet included the project description, leader and team members, deliverables, project benefits, estimated value (ROI), methodology, timeline, and cost. Getting our boss's buy-in for the budget and list prioritization was Mission One. Assembling highly skilled experts was Step Two.

Commitment and drive are two of the most important qualities I seek out when I select team members to join me on collaborative projects. My work experience has shown a project is doomed to fail without the dedication and sense of urgency of team members.

I love to laugh and do so out loud in meetings because being joyful rubs off on others. Possessing a positive attitude and having faith that colleagues and projects will achieve high success is the *modus operandi* that I find works the majority of the time.

Finally, losing my sister and best friend would have diminished my happiness for the rest of my life. The emotional trauma I endured gave me a perspective that frames my work and home life. I strive to design my days with the above eight principles in mind.

Life is simply too precious.

Ellen Glassman recently received the YWCA's Tribute to Women in Industry award. If you go into any Target store, you'll find a designer collection of electronics for women named after Ellen's daughter, Liv.

DISCOVERY

FINDING THE COURAGE TO CHOOSE

"I have more steel in me
than I had ever imagined."

• • •

"I felt like a ton of bricks were lifted from my
shoulders...free...because I was being true to
myself."

• • •

"Work is a verb, not a place.
Don't sell yourself short."

• • •

"We were transformed that night
and my view of myself, of others, will never be the same."

The highest level of courage — like standing up to a
horrible injustice — is obvious to us all. But saying "No"

to your boss; or speaking out;
or pushing beyond your current skills;
or walking away from overtime;
or finding a better job;
or just ignoring the deluge of emails,
also require an everyday
kind of courage.

• • •

Most every letter-writer discovered
that once they found inner clarity,
courageous choices that once seemed
difficult became easy.

• • •

Crackling clarity, deep clarity
changes everything.
Awareness changes the outcome.
You can focus
on what really needs doing;
surrender to a higher calling;
claim the garbage that is yours;
give and receive more graciously;
create more intimacy;
get balanced;
follow your longings;
live life out loud;
do or be whatever you wish.

• • •

You have the steel and compass you need
within you.

• • •

Your biggest barrier is not lack of courage.
It's blowing past the fog.

Find the Courage to Cast Off the Mantle of Work

John Santoro

Work: Living life to the fullest for his daughter

John Santoro is Executive Director, Leadership Communications for Pfizer. He works with the company's chairman on communications strategy and execution. He also has overall responsibility for Pfizer's Annual Report. He's writing to his son, Michael, 14 years old.

DEAR MIKE,

I am writing this at the national meeting of Compassionate Friends. All of us — you, me, and Mom — are sadly members of this organization, devoted to those who have lost children and siblings. Our Paula — your twin — left us on December 10, 2000, at age 10, from the complications of Cushing's Syndrome. Few people have ever heard of this disease. We know it painfully well.

We come to these meetings not only to honor Paula, but also to continue our journey through this valley of tears. I know I speak for both me and Mom, and I can try to speak for Paula, in saying that we cannot be prouder of how you managed to grow into a fine young man, despite enduring the unendurable. You're nearly 14 now, strong of body and spirit, warm-hearted, smart, funny, and talented. It is incredible to watch you play trombone and sitar with skill and passion. Your music may be as important to me as it is to you. When you play, I feel almost as I did before Paula passed on. The moments without pain are fleeting, but I am grateful for each one.

I went to a seminar this morning called For Men Only. Two dozen guys, from all walks of life, talking about the unthinkable. Most of the sharing was wrenching and poignant, but some of it was comical — like our almost-maniacal devotion to work, even in the face of tragedy. We spoke of the intersection of work and grief — that somehow, in the middle of the worst event that could ever happen to us and our families, our thoughts turned to our "To Do" lists. One man spoke of going back to the office two days after his 22-year-old daughter died, even before her funeral was held. He didn't know why, he just had to go. I wasn't quite that way after Paula died, but one of the first phone calls I made on that dark Saturday of her passing was to my boss, at home. I began going through all my projects, one-by-one. He was stunned and fighting back tears. I had the calm demeanor of a man rightly in shock. Two days later I took the car in for service. It was due.

Paula lived a life under constant stress. The hallmark of Cushing's Syndrome is a set of adrenal glands gone haywire, pumping out much more cortisol than the body wants or can use. Cortisol is a "flight or fight" hormone. Paula's body told her that her world was always in chaos.

She adapted to her body's screwed-up signaling by trying to control every aspect of her activities. Each day began with a checklist, finely handwritten, with sharply drawn checkboxes. All her possessions were arranged in precise rows. She was a walking

Palm Pilot, who could unfailingly remind you of appointments made or library books due. When she started a project, be it a poem or a picture, there was no stopping her until it was complete. She was literally driven by her disease to perfection.

Yet Paula had remarkably modest career aspirations. She could read stock charts at age eight, but all she wanted to be was a store clerk or a letter carrier. She cared about others much more than she cared about herself. The plight of the poor and the fate of the Earth were very much on her mind, even at that tender age.

Our mementos of Paula are her work outputs — dozens upon dozens of detailed drawings and poems with metaphors so startling that it's hard to believe they were composed by a preteen. Our house is teeming with these elaborate artworks. We are grateful that she was so prolific in expressing herself.

Yet my fondest memories of Paula are found in the times she could cast off the mantle of work. A week before her body delivered its final betrayal, we watched "America's Funniest Videos." Paula loved slapstick humor and she laughed so hard I was afraid she'd burst the surgical stitches in her abdomen. It was the last time we would really share her famous belly laugh. One week later, she belonged to the ages.

And then there was June 2000, just a few months before Paula entered the hospital. Along with everything else in our lives, my company, Warner-Lambert, was bought by Pfizer in a transaction that started on less than positive terms. When it turned friendlier, I was asked to help on the transition team, and ultimately joined Pfizer, in large measure due to their compassion after Paula's passing. The first half of 2000 was a time of great upheaval in my work life. I was looking forward to a long-planned family vacation to Disney World.

I scheduled that vacation for long past the most pessimistic estimates of when Pfizer would close the deal on Warner-Lambert. As fate would have it, Day One of the new Pfizer was the day we were set to leave. I was asked to consider postponing my vacation, just for one day, and decided not to. We left as planned for what would become the last vacation we would take together, at least on this earth.

At Disney World, we asked you and Paula to tell us one thing you wanted to do above all else. For you, it was a ride on Space Mountain. For Paula, it was perhaps the lowest-tech activity you can do at Disney — visit the home of Minnie Mouse. I remember her excitement about the whimsy of the house of a fictional mouse. She laughed and laughed, that belly laugh again.

I now get to Orlando quite often on business. Every time, I make it a point to visit what is now, to me, sacred ground...Minnie's House.

My first few times back there, I'd break down in tears, sometimes so violently that people would give me the "Madman's Berth." Things are better now. I still weep at the Magic Kingdom, but I am also grateful for the memories of being there as a family in June 2000. My company was gone, my career uncertain, my life about to change in ways I could not fathom, and still don't. For 30 glorious shining minutes, though, Paula saw her beloved Minnie's home, poked around in her refrigerator, and walked in her garden. She threw off her mantle of work, and, on that day, let me do the same.

Remember that day as you build your career. Hard work is noble, but nobler still is knowing when to put it aside, and savor the love and warmth of family, to whom I know you will give your best.

Love, Dad

John Santoro lives in New Jersey but is often on the road. He cheers Michael on in sitar competitions (this blond kid from the burbs wows the Indian community), and Boy Scout overnights and volunteer activities.

• • •

Have the Courage to Say Yes to Your Dreams

Caroline Simonds

Work: Helps others live, die, and see the value of a smile

Caroline Simonds practices pediatric care in a very unique way in eleven hospitals throughout France. She employs 48 professional clowns. She is writing to her goddaughter, Yanny.

DEAR YANNY,

In a week you will turn six. When you were only three, you lost your momma and are now in a boarding school in Shanghai, China. I sit in my apartment in Paris, hoping someday to help guide you into adulthood, through work, and beyond. Since we are so far apart, maybe this letter will give you a few appetizers from my heart's cupboard.

Lying in bed, your momma invited me to be your godmother. Fairy godmother would probably better define me! But your mother knew I would always be there for you.

Yanny Jacqueline Wang, learn to say yes to your dreams. Then measure your risks, and trust serendipity to guide you. Let me explain...

I went to college and got a degree in music and theatre. I was expected to go on to graduate school and become either a composer or a professor. Wrong.

I took all my savings (from go-go dancing in a hunting lodge in upstate Vermont, and teaching flute at $5 an hour) and took off for my dream city — Paris! I was 22 years old. Within four weeks I fell madly in love with a brilliant street acrobat with a Ph.D., met a theatre director who wanted to recruit me for his school, connected with a modeling agency, and started orchestrating music for cartoons at "La Maison de la Radio."

Four clear paths presented themselves to me: Run away with the circus and make no money; go to Strasbourg and get a Master's degree in theatre; make a ton of cash modeling fancy furs and wearing high heels; or pursue a career in composing music with my first paying job. Guess what I chose? I followed my heart and joined an incredible baroque street circus: "Le Palais de Merveilles" (The Palace of Wonders). For the next ten years, from one village in France to the next, I was known as Lili Ratapuce.

I went back to the U.S. in 1980 with my newborn baby, Lailah. Again, I had no money. But within a few years, I had built a career as a freelance celebration artist, performing for the rich, the modest, and the poor. Some days I dressed up as a mermaid. Other days, I impersonated the Statue of Liberty. And on others, I wore shimmering iridescent blue wings. In the fancy hotels of Manhattan and in the schoolyards of Brooklyn, they all called me Dragonfly.

It was all wonderful! But Yanny, the work that changed my calling was becoming a "clown-doctor" for the Big Apple Circus Clown Care Unit. We visited hospitalized children twice a week, all year round. Some kids had life-threatening illnesses like cancer and heart disease. Others had been shot in street fights. For three years, I grew more than I had during the rest of my life. And because attitude is so critical to wellness, I contributed to the lives of many others.

Then, I found that my dreams outgrew what I could accomplish with the Big Apple Clown Care Unit. The most difficult choice I ever faced in my working life was to change things while they were still going well. I decided to reinvent what I had learned under my own vision.

I went back to Paris. Made hundreds of calls. Wrote hundreds of letters. Met dozens of people. When the first of many grants came in, my husband, Patrick, and Lailah left New York to join me.

I now direct a company of 48 performers — Le Rire Medecin (The Laugh Doctors). We work in 11 hospitals all over the country and make over 40,000 individual visits with sick kids each year.

Twice a week, you'll find me, "Dr. Giraffe," in a huge cancer hospital in the suburbs of Paris.

Recently, when I came back from my summer break, I discovered that we had lost 20 kids. This means that my brown-eyed Olivier, mischievous Charlotte and Pierre, the poet Shirley, the philosophical Maude, Oscar, Melanie, and Sami from Lebanon are gone. Daily, I think of their families. I will never get used to the grief I must live with, yet I have learned to accept that the work I do makes a difference in the moment. Those moments add up to minutes and then to a lifetime. If we can all still see the value of a smile, then maybe we'll all be OK.

All those moments, and all those smiles, and all those changed lives were possible because a dragonfly learned to say yes to her dreams.

You are still too young to worry about going to work and making brow-wrinkling decisions. But when you do, I will be close by. For now, let's celebrate life together. I'll be there for your first taste of champagne, and to give you a bottle of my Vetiver perfume.

Please make me laugh when I am an old clown!

I love you, Caroline

To her dearest friend, **Caroline Simonds** will always be a 6 foot 1 inch dragonfly with purple hair, who occasionally needs to borrow grown-up clothes to speak at conferences. She's co-author of *The Clown Doctor Chronicles,* which tells the story of the amazing resilience of individuals she has seen under the most debilitating of circumstances. Since she wrote this letter, Yanny has moved to Long Island, New York, to live with her 48-year-old half-sister.

Must Compliance
Be the Name of the Game?

Feir Johnson

Work: Living, loving, enjoying life to its fullest

Feir Johnson is a musician, writer, and retired teacher. She wrote curriculum for Grades 7 and 8 for Ontario, Canada, public schools, has one degree in music, another (for fun) in interior decoration, and is currently studying for her doctorate in hypnotherapy.

HELLO NEW TEACHER,

I seldom see you in the staff room or even the parking lot. But at staff meetings I notice you have that overexhausted look of all new teachers. The only thing I can compare the exhaustion to is that of a medical intern. Even so, interns have it better. When they go home from 12-hour shifts they don't take work with them.

So here you are, maybe idealistic, maybe not, freshly armed, you think, with new ways of teaching. During practice teaching, you learned what you will or won't do. You have a game plan.

After your first month, did your game plan turn to crap? Did you find that the constant attention required by the two behavioral-problem students in your class, the magazine sales, the absences for sporting events, the P.A. announcements, had punctured those carefully prepared methods you were so sure of?

Have you found that the dysfunction of

students' families often keep you late after school (good preparation and marking time) so you can hear about your personality conflict with a student who's a nonachiever? When it comes to getting support from that dysfunctional parent, and getting your government-enforced curriculum taught, have you found that your colleagues are often absent, or question your methods, playing the P.R. game? And all this before your second month on the job.

The other day you came into my classroom as I was marking. The lights were on. It was dark in the unlit parking lot. (We hope that sometime soon women teachers' safety becomes an issue at a board meeting.) I still had an hour's work to do, but I listened.

The letter you were sending to a parent concerning her child had not been presented to the principal for approval before you sent it. You were sternly lectured. Your work as a journalist in the business world, your Master's Degree in English, were disregarded by the feudal system of authority. When, you asked me, did elementary teaching demand that you behave like a child in a strongly paternalistic family? Did you sign over your rights as an adult when you became an elementary teacher?

You're very apologetic asking for my time. (You have now realized what a precious commodity a teacher's personal time is.) But you don't think you can take this anymore. I seem different from the others. I seem to have dissociated myself from them, and "walk to the beat of my own drum." None of the others seem to welcome questions or even yourself into their classrooms (little fiefdoms). The few times you have put some well-reasoned questions to them they appeared uncomfortable.

Well, I say, you've entered the hypocritical world of elementary education. In this world, thoughtful challenge receives lip service but no commitment, and uniformity (conformity) is the desired outcome. This is an area where the "individual learner" is encouraged and the "individual teacher" is not. Leadership courses are recommended for the best of conformists, or as a perk for the teacher appearing a little too "individual." What is taught in them is not practiced. Does the truth appear negative, I ask? Well, yes, it is.

You leave my room thinking I'm a jaded, bitter teacher, passed over for promotion, or with serious emotional issues. Yet what has drawn you to me is my evident passion for good education. You see a person who has found her joy within the classroom, who likes to help others do so as well, and journeys into the external world only when her students' interests are involved. What I've told you and who I am doesn't compute. In spite of your respectable educational background you can't internalize this truth. You rationalize me.

You've come to the great divide in your career as a teacher. Will you create a feudal fiefdom, or will you dissociate, become something of a border state? Is this choice necessary? Is there another way?

It's Christmas, and you're back. Your friend has just walked out the school door and is never coming back. Should you do the same thing? You are trying

to write the government-demanded computer
reports (three hours extra work each night at school,
after school), help me with the Christmas (oops!
Holiday) Concert, and you've just heard that the
principal doesn't like your precise comments about
why Johnny can't do the work. The principal prefers
you change "Johnny never does his homework and
does not complete classroom assignments due
to excessive socializing" to "Johnny finds focusing
himself on the work at hand challenging.
Organizational skills need to improve."

This isn't the truth. You've been asked to
sanitize and politically correct-ize an evaluation,
to obfuscate. What to do?

I point out that you are in your probationary
year. If you wish to stay, compliance is the name of
the game. You need to put aside your integrity until
you have a permanent contract. Put it aside carefully,
so you may bring it back when you have some years
of experience.

I see this is really unpalatable to you. You tell
me so. But you also tell me that your earlier opinion
of me has grown — you've found that some staff
members speak highly of my help. And you note that
I've been a Thinking Strategies consultant. Thanks.

After that, just when things are under control,
you are sucker-punched. You meet me at a personal
conference booth where we imbibe scotch and I
spout survival truths.

"What is this?" you ask, waving a brown
envelope. You've received a letter of reprimand.
You've transgressed. How? The letter says you are

using confusing teaching techniques. Your dysfunctional parent has hit again. "What confusing techniques," you ask, "I just used some new ones from the book I've been reading." You tell me these methods really work. You're excited about them. You see some of your students really sparking with them. Maybe there's joy in teaching after all. Now this.

So...comes my *veritas*. To endure, an intelligent, aware, passionate teacher, you must:

- **Know yourself and how you fit into the system —** square pegs can find square holes.
- **Choose your issues,** where you can preserve your integrity.
- **Keep reading, learning, doing,** even when others don't.
- **Love passionately** what you do with children.
- Learn to do new methods **subversively.**
- **Document everything,** especially your programs.
- **Be your own cheering section —** external sources are very unreliable.
- **Seek mental help** if you feel yourself burning out. It is no longer a firing offense (as it was 20 years ago) to have mental health needs.
- **Use your union to protect you** when your superior's ignorance threatens you harm.

Now it's the last day of school. You help me carry things to my car. You are going to your first of many summer courses to further your teaching knowledge. You feel stronger. You've weathered this year, and made personal choices about your life. You even know what you will be teaching and where you will be teaching as of September. (Subject to immediate change. Sorry, but you had to know this.) We say goodbye with plans to look in on each other during our time off.

You drive off seasoned, excited by the year to come. I drive home, retired — early.

Feir Johnson asks and answers, "Do square pegs feel like square pegs? I don't think so. I never have, nor should other workers with a strong sense of self and a wide outlook. The trick is to keep that inner-self surviving by creating, doing, and giving."

• • •

Inner Voices
Journey Notes from the Gut

You Have More Steel Inside You Than You Know
Perhaps the biggest decision I will make today is whether I will get out of bed. I certainly don't feel up to the challenges that today is going to bring me. But I suppose that's the price I pay for taking the biggest risk of my life.

When I first came to New York after graduating college, I thought that everything was going to be okay. Well, it wasn't. For six months, I was unable to find a job, and my husband's inadequate income was all there was. Growing up middle class, I never knew what it was like not to have money to buy a loaf of bread. The point arrived where we were eating nothing but rice.

I took a job just for the money. The boss allowed people he favored to show up drunk for work, do an incompetent job, or not show up at all. Those he didn't like (me) were violently berated for doing things like not putting in 12-hour days. I had to quit. After all, integrity can't be bought and sold, and once it's gone, there's no way to get it back. Money, and especially jobs, are a different matter.

I have no way to see whether the business my husband and I ended up starting will succeed or fail, but I know that when I look back on this messy, chaotic, painful year, I will have learned a whole lot about work and money and where they fit in my life. I have learned that life is not always fair, and that sexism and ageism are still big problems.

Yet, perhaps most importantly, I have learned that I have more steel in me than I had ever imagined.

— **Sara Gillis** is 23 years old. She and her husband now run a mortgage company with five employees, and growing.

• • •

It's Quitting Time!

Debbie Rech

Work: Nurturing relationships wherever she goes, whatever she does

Debbie Rech's career includes stints in large retail chains, reporting for a small-town newspaper, and desk-clerking at the local gym. The common thread: Observing and loving the idiosyncrasies of humankind.

TO ALL THOSE WHO WORK,
Today is the day I've been thinking about for roughly

seven months. I've been with this company for eight months.

Today I get to hand my boss my two weeks notice, and put this experience behind me.

I've left other companies before — usually for a better opportunity. In this case, I am just leaving.

Sure, the uncertainty is troublesome. Like anyone, I have bills that need to be paid. However, the fear of the unknown is better than the reality of the known with this job.

This job has literally made me sick. I am normally a healthy person and rarely take sick time. In this job, I not only had to use all my sick days, I almost had to use a week's worth of vacation to cover for my recent bout of mono. Mono!

I view my lack of wellness as a Dis-Ease. In this case, it couldn't be more obvious. It's my job. And, the only way I can return to good health — mentally and physically — is to leave.

For me, this position — as an Assistant Manager in a retail store — should have been easy. It's retail, not rocket science. You serve the customers, you do the paperwork, you go home at the end of the day. But my supervisor made it painfully difficult. She lied, she encouraged tattle-taling among coworkers, she was hung over more days than not, and she didn't care about me, as a person. The latter was the final straw for me.

How do you have an employee out sick with mono and only bother to call her to tell her she needs to bring in a doctor's note when she returns?

Although I expected as much — based on all of

her subhuman behaviors since the beginning — the reality of her poor treatment made me say "Enough is enough."

As my doctor so brilliantly stated, "Life's too short to put up with that shit."

So heeding the doctor's advice, I will be handing my supervisor my doctor's note along with my two weeks notice.

On to better things.

Debbie Rech couldn't be better. Since writing her letter, she became special events manager at a public broadcasting station, and hasn't used a sick day since saying *sayonara* to that subhuman boss.

• • •

Find the Courage to Learn What Doesn't Matter

Peter Tunjic

Work: Being a happy lawyer with a soul

Peter Tunjic is many things: a father, commercial lawyer, amateur philosopher, and enthusiast.

DEAR PARTNERS,

Please accept my resignation from the practice.

I'm sure many of you will be relieved by my decision, as I have not been a model employee.

Since I began my career as a commercial lawyer with the firm many years ago, I have learned much about the business of law. Unfortunately, from the perspective of the partners, I appear to have learned all the wrong things:

I was meant to learn that the firm values time. To record my daily activities in six-minute units, to manage my time effectively, and ultimately to sell time.

> **Instead,** I learned that my time has no value to the partners. I came to learn to be generous with my time, and to ignore the notional value placed on it. By doing this, my practice became fueled by unfettered curiosity, and grew in ways I could never have intended.

I was meant to know our business — the law. To attend professional seminars, read professional journals, and write professional papers.

> **Instead,** I learned that knowing the law in the absence of its context made the practice of law meaningless to me, and irrelevant to our clients. I learned to seek the company of those outside the law, to read more philosophy than law, to attend seminars with no immediate connection to the firm or the law.

I was meant to work exclusively for the firm. The law was meant to be my job.

> **Instead,** I learned that I work for many people, organizations, and networks. The law and the firm may pay the bills — but the work I do for the networks I have established, the universities I lecture in, and the individuals I mentor provide other forms of payment or returns, including

connections, reputation, knowledge, and experience beyond anything the firm alone could ever provide. I now have more to trade than technical skill and money.

I was meant to learn that the work I do for the firm today creates my opportunities for work tomorrow.

Instead, I learned that tomorrow I walk not into the consequences of today, but of all my days. This is likely to make no sense to you, but is fundamental to the way I have come to be in the practice of law and business. In essence, I learned that the best commercial strategy for my tomorrows is to be present at all times today.

I was meant to understand the mechanics of business, and to learn to rely on my intellect — to outthink each problem, and make critical judgments.

Instead, I have come to learn that business is too complex to rely solely on intellect and the mind. The messiness of business requires additional strategies. I have learned that my mind must ultimately navigate the oceans created by my behavior. Spending time in silence, reflection, and contemplation of what I stand for has changed my behavior and now the context in which I practice the law. This is my principal strategy for working in the mess and bringing congruence to the complexity. I have further learned the importance of avoiding judgment. I prefer to be mindful of the complexity, and aware that the longer I suspend judgment, the more open I become to the deeper causes and consequences of what is happening in both the way I practice the law and the way business is conducted today.

I was meant to have a business plan and a strategy. Instead, I have come to learn how "unwise it is to wander about in times that do not belong to me." I have come to realize I will never be what I am now in this moment. This is my business plan and my strategy. And by design or coincidence, I have gone, in a short amount of time, from being an unhappy, mediocre lawyer, to a happy lawyer whose counsel is sought by great leaders, innovators, and strategists. Curiously, I never sought any of these clients. Put simply: The more I practiced what I had come to learn, to devalue six-minute increments of my time, to seek a diversity of connections, to be present, practice mindfulness and avoid planning for the future — the more interesting my work became, and the more opportunities emerged for me, both personally and professionally.

Reading this, many of you may feel vindicated in your views that I simply disagree with your views as a matter of course. For my part, this has never been my intention. In fact, it is not that I disagree with what you have learned about the business of law. From where you stand, what you have learned, and now seek to practice, makes eminent sense.

I know that our relationship has not been easy for you, and that you have been incredibly tolerant of my learning disability. But tolerance is not the foundation of a relationship, and for all I have learned, I have not learned how to change the way you think. I wonder if this can ever be learned. I suspect it can't.

All I can do is practice what I now know, and have faith that by doing this, I will continue to be happy and surprised by what comes my way.

Yours Faithfully.

In all that he does, **Peter Tunjic** is present, generous of spirit, and intensely curious. He now runs Thoughtpost Legal, writing great stories (contracts) for uncommon clients from his home in Victoria, Australia.

• • •

Find the Courage to Never Pretend

Cheryl Backlund

Work: Leading others in how she supports them

Cheryl Backlund has been working at Cisco in San Jose, California, for almost eight years. Until recently, she was an Administrative Assistant in the Corporate Marketing department. She's now a full-time mommy.

DEAR LILLY,

As I write this letter, I'm seven months pregnant with you. The idea that you will one day be making a living for yourself is a little hard to grasp right now, but before we know it, you'll be facing the excitement and challenges of the working world.

As you enter that world, you may see what you're doing as just another day at work, just another meeting or discussion or project that you need to get done. But all those days, meetings, projects and discussions are masquerading as lessons.

I have always seen myself as a follower and was most comfortable as a follower. But in this job, the people I work for see me as a leader — a great Administrative Assistant — because I know how to get things done quickly and efficiently. It shocks me that they see me this way. But because I exude self-confidence, I'm called a leader.

Being a leader is new to me. Looking back at my past jobs, I realize that it was obvious to my coworkers and bosses that I was a follower. That's what I did best, what I knew how to do. It wasn't a negative thing. I was a good employee, and did what I was told to do, and was appreciated because of that.

My switch came when I joined Cisco. Everyone around me had a technical background and I was scared because I didn't. To keep up, my manager had me take a course: Cisco Business Essentials for Non-Technical People. Two hours into it, everything was going completely over my head. Of course, I didn't want anyone to know. I would look bad, I was embarrassed. So I pretended to be interested and pretended to be learning.

Back at my job, I felt like an imposter. My manager was urging me to take on a more technical role, but that wasn't what *I* wanted. I told him that I was happy being an administrative assistant and didn't enjoy classes that would turn me into someone else. And that's when I began to act like a leader.

I felt like a ton of bricks were lifted from my shoulders...free...because I was being true to myself.

Lilly, my dear daughter, with that one admission — when I decided not to pretend anymore and listened to my heart about the direction I wanted my work to take — my self-confidence changed from low to high, and I was truly happy.

I want you to feel the same thing — be true to yourself, and be happy with your choices. Take a risk if it means that risk will bring you to the level of comfort and happiness you deserve. Self-confidence and comfort go hand-in-hand. If you have self-confidence, you will be comfortable, and if you are comfortable, the self-confidence will shine through — and your coworkers and bosses will see that.

You have the inner power and strength to take whatever career path you wish, and make whatever career choices you want. Knowing that you listened to your heart will give you a sense of self that will stay with you, no matter what you are doing, for the rest of your life.

Love, Mommy

Since writing her letter, **Cheryl Backlund**, 34, is now beaming as a proud mom. "It has been so amazing to watch Lilly transform from a newborn into a girl who chatters up a storm! Her favorite word right now is "AAAAAHHHHHHH!!!!!" Enjoying motherhood so much, she and her husband are expecting the arrival of Lilly's new brother.

Inner Voices
Journey Notes from the Gut

Work With Those Who Work On Themselves

The people I have been able to learn from taught with their very being, with their entire selves. They also, one and all, were learning right alongside of me. All of my teachers were also students. They were people who ventured forth into the great unknown. They embraced questions. They tackled mysteries: "Who am I? Why am I here? What do I serve?" Their work was to work on themselves. In the process, others were affected. I am one of those.

I don't think it matters what one does for work, but what does matter, for me, is that the work is able to sustain an ever-increasing interest; that the work leads in unexpected directions; that it unveils me unto myself. I can tell I am heading on the right path when my work brings me closer to a valuation of life in all its forms. When this happens, I feel accountable for the work I do. It becomes more than me and I feel responsible to it. When I feel responsible, I sense how much I've yet to learn. And I burn to continue.

In the end, we are all individuals. You must find your own work, a work that is greater than your self. When you find it, you will suffer. When you suffer, you will seek help, and you will grow. When you grow, others will grow along with you.

— **Matt Mitler** was originally trained in humanistic and existential psychology before discovering the healing potential of theater. He is director of Theatre Group Dzieci (Polish for "Children"), which is committed to combining art and service as a path for transformation.

Inner Voices
Journey Notes from the Gut

Never Hang Back, Wedge Yourself Forward

Years ago, as a widowed mother with two young children, the idea of work took the form of a cage or a boa constrictor: *I have to support my children. I have to work, unceasingly, for the rest of my life because no one else is going to take care of us!*

But I love work. I hope you will too. Not for the money or the perks, but because it offers a place to express yourself to a captive audience.

Work is a verb, not a place. A business is simply where I go to do my work, but I'm working most all the time. This matters a lot: Identify your God-given talent, cherish it, refine it, and then find a way to get paid for it for as long as you need to.

The most important thing is connecting with a place that is big enough for your talents, with people you enjoy and can learn from. No matter what your responsibilities, use every opportunity to wedge your talents into the forefront. Make suggestions. Design a solution and put it in front of the CEO as "just something to think about." Invent the need for what you deliver. Express yourself. Chances are that people will start to pay attention, especially since so many people just hang back and do what they're told.

Don't sell yourself short.

— **Cass Cannon** originally held a number of jobs consistent with her English degree — waitress, woodcutter, and bartender — and 20 years later ended up as a Performance Improvement Coach for the University of Virginia Health Services Foundation.

Have the Courage to Find What You're Losing

Paul Mackey

Work: Helping others develop their ability to adapt, as he develops his own

Paul Mackey recently left a 30-year career as an auditor, real estate planner, financial manager, and organizational strategist with the Canadian Government to start his own practice. He is finding it anything but comfortable — and loves it! He's writing to his wife Patti and his four daughters: Sara, 22 years old, Rebecca, 21, Christina, 18, and Joelle, 17.

DEAR FAMILY,

As a teenager, I learned that hard work was a way for me to hide from strong emotions. Since then, when feeling jilted, frustrated, or confused, I could immerse myself in deadlines, work up a good sweat, strive to achieve clear, measurable goals, and then reward myself with the inner satisfaction of achievement.

The exhilaration of accomplishment made me forget the emotions that had driven me to work hard. The concentration required to meet business challenges diverted my attention from what I was feeling to what I was doing. When the emotions of inadequacy arose, I had a simple answer: Work harder, learn faster, and focus more!

What impact did this have on me? It brought success, promotions, recognition, and self-confidence. Everything seemed to validate the idea that repression of emotion through work was a winning formula.

This is probably why it took years to realize

what I was losing in the process.

A turning point was changing jobs. I remember saying to you, "Gee, I didn't realize how much that old job was draining from me." It hit me like a body check when you answered, "We did!"

Reflecting back on the symptoms, I developed some remote sensing — ways to flag to myself that I needed to pay attention. For example, if I found myself constantly walking into the office thinking "What business could I start?" I recognized this as a signal to seriously examine how I was feeling about my work and to act on those feelings.

Another signal was to recognize when I was feeling comfortable. Attaining comfort is not the goal! In fact, it is the opposite. Goals stretch us, while comfort works against those stretches. I was comfortable playing with ideas, and teaching and developing others. I felt great when I was learning, creating new approaches, recognizing the complexity and the chaos. I was fascinated with change, thirsted after opportunities to influence change and to parti-cipate in bringing concepts to life. On the other hand, I was uncomfortable with personal change which required reflection, meditation, deep examination of personal values, and in taking risks which might damage the sense of self I had established through hard work. It was easier to commit to an idea than to personal change. I was more comfortable seeking the Aha's than recognizing the Oh-oh's.

Now, as I make the leap from being an employee of a large organization, to being a free agent, I have come to realize, perhaps more than ever, that being uncomfortable is a desirable state, essential to learning, essential to strong relationships and essential for deep change. Without the feelings of unease and uncertainty, I don't grow. Without growth, I have less to contribute.

Thankfully, I have had you, to shake me out of the office mindset, to question me, to help me think about what matters, and to support me as I seek answers.

Love, Dad

One of **Paul Mackey's** fulfilled dreams is working on the family's second home in France, "a 300-year-old building that needs about 25 years of renovation and repair. Even though we love the place, it is our friends and family who gather there that keep us going back. It is where we make time for reflection and inquiry. We live in Ottawa, yet we really come alive in France."

• • •

Have the Courage to Turn Fears into Excitement

Mike Grabowski

Work: Helping people confront their fears

Mike Grabowski is a director of human resources for ARAMARK Corporation. He's writing to his children, Andrew, 7 years old, Maggie, 5, and Sophie, 3.

TO ANDREW, MAGGIE, AND SOPHIE,

The fire raged and 10-foot flames leapt upward toward the tall pine trees around us. The heat was so intense that several times we backed away to avoid being burned. We were standing in the spot where Boy Scouts had been coming to meet for over 100 years. As I held tightly to your hand, Andrew, I looked up at the night sky and saw more stars than I can remember seeing in my life. I felt a deep sense of connection to the earth, to you, and to the fire. This was only the beginning of an extraordinary evening that transformed me at the deepest levels.

After the fire had burned for about 90 minutes, the woman leading the walk raked the coals into a flat bed about ten feet long. I could feel the intense heat on my face and arms. After a few moments she said, "The fire is now open." You were only five at the time, but you had more courage than I did as we both removed our shoes and prepared to cross the coals. I kept looking over at the woman for some kind of disapproving look or comment. Surely you were too young to do this. It's impossible. She looked at us, seemed unconcerned, and then looked away.

We held hands and walked across 800° coals. Then we walked together again. Then we danced together across them. By your fourth walk you said, "Dad, can I go with a friend instead?" We were transformed that night and my view of myself, of others, and the world will never be the same.

The firewalking experience taught me lessons that continue to have an impact in my life. Fear is a powerful force and the biggest obstacle preventing people from achieving their goals. I've seen it lots of times at work — the look on someone's face when his whole world was taken away because of downsizing.

I could tell he was thinking: "This is all I have, now what am I supposed to do?" You see, children aren't the only ones who are afraid of things. It's OK to be afraid, it's human nature. What I learned at the fire is that you don't have to stay afraid, it's your choice. The goal is not to eliminate fear, but rather to continue to walk forward in life in spite of your fears.

Children, you have the power to turn fear into excitement! How do you do it? The best way is to find something you love and then build a career around that passion. Throughout my career, lots of people talked about the importance of doing this but never explained why. Now I know. Being passionate about what you're doing will turn fear into excitement and that will propel you past future fears.

There is one other key requirement: Keep breathing! All mammals, including humans, stop breathing when they are in fear. It happens in the jungle, the rainforest, and at work. It's amazing how many times I see this in work meetings. Someone is being questioned about a decision he or she made and stops breathing, in fear. I've asked friends to watch for this at their workplaces. They tell me it's amazing how often this happens. When you are confronting a fear that is keeping you from achieving, remember to keep breathing. Taking deep breaths will help you move forward with your fears as you turn them into excitement to achieve great things.

I spend a good deal of my time trying to attract talent to join my company. Firewalking taught me that the most important quality in a candidate is passion for what he does and who he is. This passion will drive people to succeed even when obstacles occur in the workplace. Workplace politics, naysayers, and bad bosses will not stop them from succeeding. For my money, give me someone with passion. We can teach him the rest.

Another way to turn fear into excitement is to challenge your limiting belief system. If you break those beliefs, a transformation occurs within you. Standing in front of red-hot coals, I guarantee your belief system is telling you not to cross the bed. I remember thinking, "There is no way I am going to walk over that fire because I know I will get burned....I am a bad parent for even allowing Andrew to be here....He's going to get hurt...."

The key is overcoming the belief that walking across anything is impossible. What I've learned to share with each of you is the same as I share with work colleagues: Surround yourself with people and situations where you're likely to challenge a belief system you hold. This is not easy, and sometimes it's downright uncomfortable. However, it's the best way to change fear into excitement.

Children, you all have amazing lives in front of you. I promise to help you find your passion, overcome your fears, use the word *impossible* with great caution, and most of all, to keep breathing!

I love you.

Mike Grabowski is now a certified firewalk instructor and enjoys helping people confront and overcome their fears.

DISCOVERY

FINDING JOY, SERENITY,
AND FULFILLMENT

"I taste the bitterness of sweat on my face,
I am tasting the beauty of life in hardship."

• • •

"Your gut doesn't listen to reason or emotion —
it just makes noises until it's satisfied."

• • •

"Follow your hearts and dreams.
Have little time for regret and much time for laughter."

• • •

"You'll do magical things in your lives.
You need to believe that."

It's time to find the grace in most every challenge you
face, most every choice you make, most every person you
encounter. You can do it.

• • •

There is a higher level of
what really matters.
Discover it, and you'll experience
a transformational leap of
knowing yourself and connecting
to something bigger.

• • •

Keep in mind that this final
discovery is different for each of us.
One letter-writer described it as
the joy of toil and hard work,
another as the fulfillment of
giving to others,
and another as focusing on
family above all else.

• • •

What is your statement of grace?
Follow the insights here,
then listen to yourself.

• • •

You'd sacrifice a lot to find
joy and fulfillment.
Yet *sacrifice* means *to make sacred.*
What is really worth making sacred
at work, and in life?

• • •

Who do you want to be?

Taste the Beauty of Life in the Hardship

Hoang Thi Ai

Work: Fills minds as well as stomachs

Hoang Thi Ai is 19. She wrote the following while living with her mom and six brothers and sisters in a slum in Hanoi City, Vietnam.

TO ALL WHO WORK,

When the neighbors turn off their lights to sleep, that's when my mom and I wake up to make our tofu. Every day, at 1 A.M., my mom wakes me up. She says she is used to it. As for me, even though I have been doing this job for four years, the concept of getting used to it is still so far away. Every night, Mom has to call, push and pull a dozen times to wake me up. When I finally win over the sleepy genie, I start whirling the tofu machine.

Making tofu is an incredibly hard job. It takes many stages of work to produce a nice looking and good tasting tofu (soy curd). All the stages of work have to be kept in strict continuity. First, I soaked the soybeans in water the night before. Then, the next day, I put them in the mill and grind them into powder. Then I pour the powder into the machine to purify. After that, I take the soy milk out and throw away the soybean residue. After the milk is boiled, I mix it with sour water and it congeals. Finally, I put it in a mold and press it for five minutes to become tofu.

As the machine starts whirling, my mom and I start whirling like propellers too. But I have no choice, as my family is poor. My mom has told me that making tofu is a hard job, but it is a good labor. I have to do this hard work to live, but it is better than doing any bad or illegal things to live a comfortable life.

Making tofu is also difficult because it brings some sickness. I have to soak my hands so much that they become corroded and look disgusting. We also have to carry many heavy things — too heavy for women like us — such as the milk pot, the pressed ball, the tofu mold, and we have to bend our backs so much that anyone who makes tofu has back pains. My mom has to have acupuncture all the time.

After waking at 1 A.M., our tofu production is done by noon. We have a quick lunch and a wink of sleep. I go to school in the evening.

My job is like this all year round. That's why my neighbors say that my job is all about "half meal, half sleep." To me, making tofu is much more. It is about feeding my family and sending my little sisters to school. It also allows me to go to school where, after the struggle for survival, I enter a new world of knowledge. There, I study hard and dream of a better life and a new job.

Tofu has been part of my life. Making it is a struggle and a real fight where I have to win against myself, against all the difficulties that being born in poverty have brought to me. I have to fight with all the pains, the long hours, and the hard work needed to create such a beautiful and tasty thing.

When summer comes, you can see white, fresh and buttery tofu in every Vietnamese family's meals. They happily enjoy its good taste. As I start whirling with mom beside the mill, I taste the bitterness of sweat running on my face, I taste the happiness every time I sell a tofu.

I am tasting the beauty of life in hardship. It is my hope that whatever hardship you endure, you taste sweet happiness as well as the sweat. Learn to appreciate all that every opportunity can offer.

Hoang Thi Ai is a member of the Voice of Green Bees group — a youth media team of the national Radio of Vietnam which involved differently abled, orphan, street, and working children aged 12 to 20. Shortly after she wrote this work diary, her family was evicted from their house as they could no longer pay the rent. They left Hanoi City and went into the province to find work.

• • •

Learning to Dream from the Old Man and the Sea

David Dibble
Work: Helps others find meaning and purpose in their jobs

David Dibble is a former CEO. He is author of *The New Agreements in the Workplace: Releasing the Human Spirit*. Here, he writes to his three children; Steve, 28, Mike, 26, and Quintina, 20.

DEAR KIDS,

My dad was a tuna fisherman. He loved it. And I loved it too. After months away, he would return smelling of fish and full of stories of the perils on the high seas. He and his fellow fisher types would gather around a table obscured by clouds of cigar smoke and swap lies that bordered on the mythical. I believed every word and clamored for more. I remember my dad being happy and laughing a lot. His dry wit and tendency toward small practical jokes generally kept the men in stitches and the women wary.

When net fishing pulled many more tuna to the dinner table or a date with a spoonful of mayonnaise, it also pulled the pole from my father's gnarled fingers. With the $76 mortgage unpaid, no 35¢ gas for the car, and a wife and three small children to care for, my dad did the unthinkable. He borrowed money and went to work in a factory.

Something happened to my dad when he lost his trusty pole and the feel of the salt air misting crisp at first light.

Dad didn't laugh as much or tell so many jokes. He began to read more, always with a cigarette dangling from his lips or burning quietly among a pile of crumpled compatriots in an ever graying ashtray. My dad would read and dream. He called his books his "magic carpet." They would take him where he could not go.

Dad and Mom divorced right after my little sister went to college. It was just as well considering they had become like oil and seawater.

A year later the company laid him off when business turned down. After his usual coughing bout each morning, Dad looked for work every day. Soon, the coughing sounded the alarm and the cancer began to do its work. Having the heart of a tuna fisherman, he battled with everything he had.

With the battle winding down, Dad pulled me close and rasped, "David, live your dreams. The magic carpet is not in the reading about the life you want to live, but in living it." My dad died a short time later.

My dream came to me eventually, but certainly not in the way I had imagined. Through a series of mind-boggling "misfortunes," I awoke one day with an empty canvas. I had no job, no assets, and no immediate prospects. It was, indeed, a scary time for both my family and me.

However, my dad's words wouldn't leave me alone. It felt like it was now or never.

As a systems-improvement and turn-around expert, I became a consultant (teacher). My first client, a $15 million company, went from a 5% pre-tax loss to a 7% pre-tax profit in seven months. I felt great. My teaching was valuable. Word spread and additional work knocked on my door. A year later, I created a successful four-day leadership event for executives, which led to the creation of many additional trainings.

My dream was coming to me.

Was any of this easy? Frankly, the answer to this question is a big fat NO. I had to face most of my worst fears. What about security? How will we pay the rent? Haven't you heard about starving artists, teachers, and writers? Yes. I have.

But how can we ever know our dreams if we

don't try? Isn't it worse to grow old with haunting regret and questions of what might have been?

Native Americans have no word for work. There is no work life, home life or any other kind of life. Everything is life. Life is meant to be lived doing what makes our hearts sing. My dad related this basic truth to me in the most profound way. Now, I tell my children to follow their hearts and dreams. No compromise. While we may not be able to jump into what makes our hearts sing today, we can at least start the journey, yes?

I picture myself as an old man lying in a bed in a house on stilts with a thatched roof.

I hear the surf breaking on the beach in front of my cottage. I feel the salted mist waft gently through the open windows. I am dying. I look back at my life and see that I have lived my life pulling big fish from the sea and telling stories. I have laughed and brought much laughter to others.

I have no regrets.

I turn to my grandchildren and say, "Follow your dreams. Do what makes your heart sing. Have little time for regret and much time for laughter. Be kind. Play a little joke or two. Do this, and your dreams will come to you."

David Dibble is 59, married to Linda for 33 years, and has always told his three kids that they could be or do anything. "Steve's a ray of sunshine in people's lives and a budding star in sales. Mike loves cars and is apprenticing with a master mechanic. Quintina is a human dynamo — I call her my little engine that could," says the proud dad. David is a spiritual teacher in the workplace. He is founder of The New Agreements Center for Enlightened Leadership. He and his family live in San Diego, California.

Do Not Go Gentle Into That Good Night

Kenny Moore

Work: Helps leaders and workers connect, work, and live

Kenny Moore is a former monk and present-day businessman improvising his way through the daily workaday grind. He's Corporate Ombudsman and Director of Human Resources for KeySpan, a Fortune 500 energy company. He's writing to his sons, Chris, 12, and Matt, 9.

DEAR CHRISTOPHER AND MATTHEW,

By all accounts, boys, you should never have been born.

After I left the monastery and returned to the world no longer as a priest, I was diagnosed with Non-Hodgkin's Lymphoma, an incurable cancer at its most advanced stage. I underwent a yearlong experimental treatment of aggressive chemotherapy and full-body radiation. After completing the regimen, the doctors gave me the prognosis: "Mr. Moore, if you live (and don't catch leukemia from the toxic treatment...) you may go on to survive. However, don't expect to have any children." The young lady I was dating at the time stood by my side and wept. In spite of the dire news, I asked for her hand in marriage. She had the bravery and love to accept. This woman went on to become your mother.

So, Chris and Matt, there's your first lesson in life. Sometimes terrible things happen. And sometimes, smack in the middle of tragedy, beautiful people show up and cause wonderful things to happen as well. Oddly enough, sometimes the two are intertwined. Occasionally Divine Providence even allows you to beat the odds, flourish and be surrounded by loving family and friends.

During your lives, you'll spend a lot of time at work. The workplace will provide you a wonderful venue to use your many talents to help others as well as for your own success. The Divine never bestows gifts solely in the service of the individual. They are always awarded for a larger purpose.

Work will also give you a chance to feel terrified and afraid. You'll try new things, create new opportunities, and take on new positions of responsibility. You'll feel at times like you're in over your head. It'll be somewhat akin to the first time you went swimming. You were terrified as well as exhilarated. While there was a period of time when you felt like you were drowning, you eventually bobbed to the top and started to kick. Work is a lot like that sometimes. I've spent many days of my business life feeling utterly petrified.

I tend to see the world from a different and nontraditional perspective. I also seek to have my ideas heard, respected, and implemented. Most of the time, this scares the hell out of me. Oddly enough, the business world seems to interpret my feelings of angst as courage. In the world of work, overcoming your fears often gets translated into a demonstration of leadership.

So success may be less about feeling secure and more about acting on your passion, independent of how you're feeling inside. Most of the time I feel personally insecure and inadequate. However, the outside business world sees me as secure and confident. Go figure. It makes little sense to me.

In both your professional and personal lives, stay close to people who exhibit passion. These are individuals who have a fire for purpose. They care deeply about life and will change the world for the better. Seek to find your own passion and play it out with flair and sparkle.

Learn to ask questions. Many of them. And never stop. Questions, more than answers, will be your thread to success and fun. It will keep you ever young and continually learning. Being curious in the business world might annoy some, but don't be deterred. I've come to believe that half of what they teach you in business school is wrong. Unfortunately, I'm just not sure which half it is.

So don't give too much credence to what you're taught. Go out and experiment on your own. Let life reveal to you what's true and what isn't. And don't spend too much time worrying about making money. Life will come back to support you in wonderful and abundant ways. Besides, work is only partly about money. It's more importantly about searching for your place in the world and cooperating with the many gifts that the Divine has bestowed upon you.

Stay close to ordinary folks. I'm forever meeting everyday workers who are impressive and inspirational. The vast majority of them don't hold high corporate positions. They are average employees who have humor, commitment, and a good dose of common sense. These are people who struggle daily with the vicissitudes of life, and they do it all with valor and a profound sense of the sacred enveloped in the common. They also just happen to be the ones who do most of the work and make the business prosper.

I'd also counsel you to spend time with the poor performers as well. They are colorful characters and seem to have more fun at work than most of the "high potential" employees I've met. They also have insight and alternative gifts to offer. More than a few of these workers have been branded as laggards, yet they seem to excel elsewhere.

One "poor performer" I met is head of his town's volunteer fire department and manages a million-dollar budget. Another woman, scorned by supervisors, has single-handedly raised a son with multiple sclerosis and happens to be the one who started the MS chapter in her neighborhood. She sits on its board. Laggards, indeed! These employees are relegated to work on the margins of corporate life yet they have valuable lessons to teach. And much of what they say smacks of the Truth.

Probably that's why Jesus spent most of his time associating with folks like this. It's where he felt most at home. It continues to be the place where revelations occur.

Use your business influence and personal wealth to help the poor. The world is full of people who have received far less than you and they'll require your assistance. You've been given much and the monetary rewards you'll receive will be copious in comparison.

This places a unique obligation upon you for which I and your immigrant ancestors will hold you accountable. Take this responsibility to heart.

Lastly, stay connected to the Divine. My years in the monastery were a wonderful preparation for life, both within and outside of the corporate world. They taught me that there's little I'm really in charge of, and that ultimately we are all "temporary" workers here on earth. Your success is conjoined to the mystery of the sacred. Stay connected to it. Nurture it and replenish it often. Your final happiness resides in cooperating with the will of the Heavenly Father.

Oh, and one final thing. You'll also endure pain and suffering. You'll be overlooked, unrecognized, and taken advantage of at times. You'll meet people who are self-serving rascals and crafty manipulators. You'll be cheated on and lied to. You will chaff at some of the restrictions imposed and blush at some of the corruption you'll witness. Don't be dismayed. That's part of the drama of good and evil that is central to life's unfolding.

As my recent heart attack reminds me, my days on this earth are numbered. So I'm not going to be around to guide you forever. But I promise to always be lovingly watching over you.

There will be times when you'll shine and other times when you'll fail miserably. Sometimes you'll live up to your ideals, and other times you'll compromise all that's right and just. It's part of the human condition and there's something sacred in the journey...and purposeful in the struggle.

Don't lose hope. Ask forgiveness often. Keep your optimism intact. And always keep moving forward.

You'll do magical things in your lives. I believe that. You need to believe it as well.

I love you, Daddy

Having dealt with both God and death, **Kenny Moore,** 56, now finds himself eminently qualified to work with executives on corporate change efforts. Kenny has always brought a sense of mischief in his dealings with those in authority — his sense of humor has served him well in life's many transitions. His secret project in the basement — just in case cancer or heart problems suddenly return — is keeping boxes of mementos and family artifacts and memories always updated, ready to pass on to his sons. Kenny is co-author of *The CEO and the Monk: One Company's Journey to Profit and Purpose.*

•••

If Your Gut Ain't Happy, Ain't Nobody Happy

Kristi Dinsmore

Work: Her career mission: To rid the world of bad bosses — one at a time

Kristi Dinsmore works in executive education, currently at Right Management Consultants. She lives in Centerville, Ohio, with her bacon-loving 113-pound Bouvier des Flandres dog.

DEAR PERSON WHO IS HUNGRY FOR THAT THING CALLED JOY,

The secret of a successful life and career can be found at the Shoney's Breakfast Buffet.

I know that sounds stupid but it's true. The expression "America is the land of opportunity" is a little like "All You Can Eat Buffet!" There are few more beautiful expressions, but the reality of both statements is there is a limit to what you can get. It all comes down to making good decisions. We all know that everything bad that can happen to you is a result of your own bad decisions.

Get in a car wreck — you made a bad decision to: drive fast, drive poorly, drive in rain/snow/wind/sun/fog/dark, or drive on that particular street at all. Get divorced — you made a bad decision to: date, date people who are rich/poor/older/younger/like you/not like you/cat people/dog people/too educated/not educated enough/drink/don't drink/drink too much/drink the wrong drink.

Bad job — well, this is just the natural result of a series of bad decisions: wrong position, wrong company, wrong city, wrong major in school, wrong school for making the wrong major attractive, wrong classes/grade point/activities in high school which resulted in the wrong school, wrong parents who filled your head with unreasonable expectations/didn't push you enough.

So how do you make good decisions and have a great life? Back to the breakfast buffet for some helpful hints!

- **Never Settle for Convenience**
  It is worth it to drive to the OTHER Shoney's. Life is too short to put up with dirty bathrooms, crusty utensils, and surly waitresses.

- **Plan Your Timing**

  Timing your arrival wrong results in a long wait, the wrong crowd, or a picked-over buffet. Everyone knows that 11:00 – 11:30 A.M. is bad because that's when the church crowds get out. Also, there will be no good bacon left after 1:30 P.M. Timing is everything.

- **Establish Priorities**

  The human body can only take so much. Determine your priority items and get those FIRST. Fruit cocktail is a poor substitute for hot blueberry compote.

- **Have Realistic Expectations**

  The pudding on a buffet is never homemade.

- **Ask for What You Really Want**

  The waitress does not magically know that you hate margarine. You have to *ask* for "real" butter.

- **Have Patience**

  Don't take the last, dried-out piece of French toast. There is hot, fresh French toast in the kitchen that will be out in a minute. Wait for the good stuff.

- **Compete Smart**

  While there is more food in the kitchen, you are hungry NOW. Do not let the very large woman in the Spandex get to the buffet before you. In fact, watch the hungry people — they have a sixth sense about when the fresh bacon will be coming out. It is noble to save some for others but stupid to get left with the Bacon Bits. Make sure it is your choice.

- **Know Your Teammates**

  Only go with people who share your purpose.
  Shoney's is not the place to find out that your
  friend is horrified by your ability to drink six
  pots of coffee. Do not invite the dieter along
  out of pity. They will make you guilty and cause
  indigestion. Friends should not make you feel
  guilty for either your talents or your vices.

- **Know Your Limits**

  If you are not careful you will find yourself
  frustrated that after consuming 34 slices of
  bacon at the Shoney's breakfast buffet you
  can't consume more. Even though there is still
  bacon left on the buffet, you will eventually
  have to ask for the check.

The truth is, good decisions are the result of learning
how to manage risk. Risk is really Opportunity. Risk
is a much scarier word than bacon.

Bad decisions are usually the result of making
the safe decision. Safe decisions are the ones that
ensure no one will question, ridicule or PAY
ATTENTION to you.

I used to work for Liz Claiborne as an account
executive. Not a lot of money but a cool job with lots
of free clothes. My bosses thought highly of me.
People envied my job. People thought I should be
happy with what I had. But I wanted more —
promotions, authority, money, prestige, choice of
job duties, freedom.

So I decided to go back to school and get my
MBA. And since I'd have to quit my job, go without

an income for two years, and have no job waiting for me when I graduated — my little voice was screaming, "Are you crazy? You're not good enough! You'll fail! You'll starve!" And everyone was giving me unsolicited advice about what a mistake I was making.

You know what? I got into Duke. I graduated. I got a six-figure job. All those "advisors"? Some got fired, some got laid off, some are still doing the same job ten years later. And no one is happier than I am.

Another truth is, most people don't want you to "go up for more bacon." They want you to be satisfied with one trip to the buffet. If you get more bacon, will there be any left for them? They'd rather the bacon all get cold than have someone get "more than they deserve." Polite people will leave bacon on the plate rather than be seen as greedy. Some of your very best friends will be nice, but others will call you a "pig" to your face.

So...what are you going to do?

The buffet is waiting.

I hesitate to give you advice but, in my experience, you should always listen to your gut in matters of bacon. Your gut can always be trusted to tell you when it wants more or when it's full. The gut doesn't listen to logic or reason or emotion — it just knows what it wants and makes noises until it's satisfied. You can spend your life making other people happy but when the gut ain't happy, ain't nobody happy.

Oh look, they're bringing out another pan of bacon! Race you to the buffet!

Kristi Dinsmore is currently watching the kitchen door for her special order of the really *primo* bacon. She eagerly awaits the day (about 24 hours after the economy turns around) when the employees of the world will create a mass exodus from deadening jobs and leave the bad bosses with the mess.

• • •

Mom's Work Lives On

Norma Elvira Carias

Work: Creating a better tomorrow for tomorrow's youth

Norma Carias lives in La Ceiba, Honduras. She is a psychologist who educates youth about the spread and dangers of HIV/AIDS, and counsels those already infected. She's writing to her mother, also named Norma.

DEAR MOMMY,

How can I say thank you for all your care and counsel all of my life?

Whenever I am asked why I do what I do, my answer is always, "Because of my mother!" Finally, and in spite of my adolescent concerns about how hard you made me work academically, I agree with your famous phrase: "If you can do 90%, then you can do 100%." Without you, who knows if I would have accomplished what I have.

I now have in front of me a little card you sent me in August 1991: "Excellent! Sensational! Number One! A wonder! Irresistible! The best!"

Those powerful words remain etched in my mind. I know I can accomplish anything, and that I should always try, because you always encouraged me to give my best.

You know that psychology was not my first career choice. Back then, my concept of life quality was the quantity of material goods that I could acquire through my work in chemistry. In short, how wrong I was. Now, I imagine how disastrous that would have been. I was not born to work for material goods and personal interest.

From my early experiences in this career, and my participation in church groups (also thanks to you), I dedicated my life to the service of others through social psychology. I have grown up knowing the power and positive effects that groups can give to the lives of others. You were always in numerous meetings, organizing support for strangers and friends and relatives alike. So it should come as no surprise that your daughter now continues your example. Thanks to your vision, I have been able to offer support and aid to those in most need, with special emphasis on the families.

A boss once said to me, "Normita, you must dream big!" And dreaming big to me meant doing large projects of benefit for the poor youth of Honduras. Now with CEPROSAF (Center for Promotion of Health and Family Aid), I give you thanks. You and your friends are part of this dream.

I feel very proud when someone hears my name and confuses me with you. That message reminds me to thank you on behalf of all those I help with HIV/AIDS in my travels.

You have taught me to give life to the others, to know that, in spite of any and all obstacles, we should not abandon the goal. You inspire me to do so much for others: The league against cancer, the church, CEPROSAF, the Global Youth Action Network, and so much more…your work has shown me if you can do it, I can also do it!

Thank you, Mom, for teaching me to grow, to share, to be of service to others, and never forget that your magical words had a great effect on my life. Who I am and what I do is thanks to you.

With love always,
Your daughter

In addition to serving those who need her in Honduras, **Norma Carias** has helped those in need throughout Latin America, the Caribbean, Europe, and the Middle East.

• • •

Inner Voices
Journey Notes from the Gut

Be Happy and Spread Happiness
I see too many people putting happiness on hold until a "Big Pay Day" further down the road, and that is something I am not willing to do. I'm not even sure that kind of day is ever in my horizon, but I enjoy a blessed life nonetheless.

Work, like life, should be about being happy, and spreading happiness. You should enjoy what you do while helping others enjoy their work as well. What better attitude to have than trying to serve others, and in doing so you are serving yourself. That is my continued goal in life. This past

Christmas, I did something that not many in my family would have expected. I wrote a personal letter to everyone (16 total) telling them how special I think they are and the qualities I admire. This brought much unexpected joy, and little could have felt better.

Live life without fear, doubt, or limitations. You are a beautiful idea of God, and there is nothing in the world you cannot achieve. Remember who your true Father-Mother is, and life will be your canvas. Take your challenges head-on and trust that you have all the tools to overcome them.

— **Travis Thomas** is community supervisor for spirituality.com, a Web community for anyone seeking a deeper understanding of his or her own spirituality in order to make a difference in the world.

• • •

Inner Voices
Journey Notes from the Gut

Believe You're Doing Something Worth Doing

I used to tease my father, calling him "Mr. Formerly," because whenever he was referenced in a newspaper article, it was full of "Penn Kimball was formerly at such and such an organization....And formerly at that one...." One time my mom woke up in the hospital after surgery and, after ascertaining that she was more or less OK, my father said, "I hope you don't mind but I just quit my job."

He had an absolute conviction that you shouldn't have to compromise where work is concerned. He took chances with jobs that weren't secure. He left jobs for ethical reasons, because they didn't allow him to be fully engaged, or sometimes just because the boss was an asshole. He always voted with his feet. But we always lived in a nice house, and seemed to have fun. So I've never felt that my father's choices caused us much hardship.

My father taught me that what's important about work is to believe you're doing something worth doing. That's the bottom line question I ask myself: Am I doing some good in the world? Am I using my life — my work — to make a difference? When I can say YES to that question, I know I'm on track.

> — **Lisa Kimball** started working with groups online in 1983, which was either prescient, or stupid, given how long it took for the technology to catch on. Her company, Group Jazz, and all their projects always include a significant "fun factor" because life is too short to wait until after work to play!

• • •

Just OK Is Perfectly OK

Mark Ritzmann

Work: Helps customers find and use their valuable information

Mark Ritzmann works in the software group for IBM. Prior to that he was a dot-com paper millionaire, who, in the end, walked away with $738. He is writing to his daughter, Lucy.

DEAR LUCY,

Follow your heart and the money will come. Do what you love. It's all great advice and people love to hear it. Everywhere I go, it seems like the conversations always turn to "What do I really want to do?"

The problem is, most of us never find an answer.

I know a lot of people who are searching, and I know only a few who have found. No one really sets out to become a Customer Service Rep, an Account Manager, a Sales Rep, or an Accountant. But that's what most of us do for a living. We just sort of end up there because, at some point, it became the best we could do.

My advice to you is don't worry if this happens to you — because it's OK.

But first, if you are one of those people who are touched by the career angel — you know what you want to do, get to do it, and succeed on your own terms — I will support and help you in every way that I can. Man, I hope things turn out like that for you.

But the odds are that they won't.

So be ready to turn the clichés around — instead of doing what you love, try loving what you do.

- **Make friends at work,** and make sure you enjoy being around them. Because you'll spend a lot of time with them. I've had bad jobs that turned out pretty good because I had good friends in the mix with me. Be close to them. Love them. You do not have to keep your distance just because you work with them.
- **Laugh at work.** A lot. Many, many funny things happen at work and you will come across many, many funny people and situations.

Notice them and laugh at them. It's even better when combined with the friends mentioned above. Nothing is more fun than going out for drinks with your coworkers and making fun of the boss.

- **Have great hobbies.** A line from a TV show: "When you're a little kid you're a bit of everything; scientist, philosopher, artist. Sometimes it seems like growing up is giving these things up one at a time." Don't give them up. You can be an accountant *and* a scientist *and* an artist. In fact, having an outside hobby will probably make you better at your job. And it will certainly make you more interesting.
- **Keep trying different things.** You can change jobs within the same company, change companies, or take classes. New things keep you energized and the more things you try, the greater the odds of finding something you love to do. Your energy makes the difference between just searching and listening for a calling.
- **Always do your best and be proud of what you do.** It doesn't matter what you do for a living. Whether you like it or not, do your best. There is no downside to doing something well. Doing it well can only make things better. And be proud. If someone you meet asks what you do for a living, answer clearly and loudly and make no excuses. If you can't, change jobs.

I don't love my job. It's OK, and it pays well. I'm still listening for my calling, but I do know what I love more than anything else in the world....I love you. So "OK and still trying" is just fine with me.

Love, Dad

While **Mark Ritzmann** works on his next goal of kayaking around Manhattan, five-year-old Lucy has a goal of her own. She wants to keep an elephant at Gracie Mansion, the official residence of the mayor of New York. It makes perfect sense because that's near her apartment so she can visit her new friend on the way to and from school, and there's always a policeman there to keep the elephant company. Her cat, Ella, will also live there to keep the mice away, because elephants are afraid of mice. To raise money to feed her elephant, Lucy is planning on selling the dung to local farmers as fertilizer.

• • •

Work Doesn't Matter

Kip Winsett

Work: It's not the work — it's you

Kip Winsett has worked as a station attendant, soda jerk, research assistant, housepainter, woodcutter, deck-hand on a yacht, seaman in the Swedish Merchant Marines, stage manager for rock concerts, waiter, restaurant manager, advertising salesman, computer programmer, software development manager, corporate systems manager, director of operations, and most recently, co-owner of a Web site development company. He's writing to his son, Austin, ten years old.

DEAR AUSTIN,

Work has never been very important to me. Most often, it's been something that I would have avoided altogether had I been able to afford to do so. For me, work is just about paying the bills, because if we can't pay the bills, life can be very unpleasant. Making enough money to survive is all that really matters to me. If I get anything else from work (a career, recognition, etc.), I look at it as gravy.

So don't let expectations about work, beyond making a living, interfere with your ability to enjoy life. Don't get too caught up in the whole work/career thing, unless you really want to.

I haven't. What has been important to me is personal experience — all aspects of it. And that's my advice to you: Don't let others force you into experiences you don't want. And don't ever feel you have to apologize for whatever experience you choose. You are entitled to choose freely for yourself, and can change your mind at any point (or many points) along the way.

When your mother and I got married, I had a job in software development and your mother worked in a doctor's office. We were living in La Jolla, California, had rather long drives to work every day, and while we lived only a few blocks from a beautiful beach, we rarely had the time to enjoy it. It wasn't a bad life, but we both wanted something different, something new and exciting.

We decided to move to Honolulu because we thought that would be really different. Our friends were amazed that we'd just pick up and go — we didn't even have jobs lined up. Well, once there, I landed a job as a software development manager, and your mom worked for an orthodontist. We had long commutes to work every day, lived near a beautiful beach, and rarely had time to enjoy it.

Other than scenery, little had changed.

At this point, I gave some real thought to what experience I wanted. One of the things I'd always wanted to do was build my own house — not just design it, or tell others what I wanted, but actually do it all myself.

Of course, I still had to pay the bills, so I took a job as a waiter, leaving my days free to pursue my dream experience. We bought a couple of acres of land in the jungle, far from anything — including electricity and phones. It took me nearly two years to finish our dream house, but when we moved in, I felt an extraordinary sense of satisfaction — far beyond anything I've ever had from a job.

Working nights as a waiter, I finally had time to enjoy that beach we were always living near — and more.

Your mom learned to dance the hula. We searched rocky beaches in the moonlight, looking for particular kinds of shells for her dancing costumes. We spent hours cloaked in the heavy scent of plumeria, making leis and garlands of ginger, ohia blossoms and ferns. We attended large family gatherings for traditional Hawaiian feasts of kahlua pig, raw fish, sea urchin eggs, and poi.

We found what we wanted — a truly different experience. And we both treasure our memories of it.

After ten years, when our Hawaiian adventure came to an end, we moved back to La Jolla, and once again I needed a paycheck. While being a waiter had paid the bills in Hawaii, that wasn't going to work back here.

I fell into a job as a warehouse manager for
a large corporation, and within a year, wound up
in a top executive position. This came about, as far
as I can tell, because I tend to be self-motivated,
reliable, and always find a way to get the job
done, no matter what.

After only a few months, this executive position
seemed perfectly designed for me — as a personal
nightmare. My actual work assignments were nebulous
(to make things better), there were lots of ugly power
games (one of the executives regularly reduced
women in his department to tears), the business
itself wasn't of much interest to me (a financial
enterprise), and I hadn't accomplished much.

I took a hard look at myself to determine what
I might change about myself, in order to learn and
grow while in a bad situation.

I realized that my typical job strategy had always
been to do my job extremely well, simply to ensure
getting the paycheck. Beyond that I wasn't interested.
I always had as little social contact as possible with
coworkers, and wasn't even much interested in them
at work. I judged the work-related games as boring,
superficial, and petty. In other words, I never really
connected with the people I worked with — I
alienated myself.

I realized that it was precisely this strategy
that was now preventing me from doing my job well.
Luckily, I also decided that I could personally benefit
by changing this.

I applied myself to learning about interacting
with others, about leading, cooperating, competing,

about the games people play, about sincerity and insecurity. I researched communication skills, management techniques, and stretched myself way beyond my personal comfort zone as a loner. As a result, I actually began to see others as real people with their own goals and hopes and fears, and I realized, for perhaps the first time, that *they saw me in terms of how I might affect them.*

I began to pay attention to other people. I talked to them, asked them about their department, what they thought it needed, how other departments could be of assistance to them, and through our discussions we discovered together what I already knew had to be done. Then when I proposed solutions, or issued policies or directives, they were ours, not mine. What a difference that made!

Ultimately, the satisfaction I got in this job was not from the job, not from the money, nor even from doing it well, but from satisfying my own needs for personal growth. It wasn't all smooth sailing — in fact it was very difficult — but when I left that company, I felt a deep sense of accomplishment, knowing that I had grown beyond the isolation from others that I had imposed upon myself for years.

What really matters at work, dear boy, is that YOU find some way to get satisfaction from it. It's so important to understand that while you can't always control what work will bring to you, you can control what you bring to it.

At any point in your life you want to be able to look back and say "Oh, that was good, that was tasty." If your work gives it to you, then count yourself lucky. If you can find that no matter what the work provides, then count yourself wise.

Love, Dad

When asked about his most precious memory of Austin, here's what **Kip Winsett** had to say: "The memories aren't of any specific events, but rather of a vulnerability he has. Up until about six months ago he would have his friends spend the night with him but was unwilling to spend the night at their house. Whenever he shows this vulnerable side of himself that is so at odds with his normal confidence I am very moved and, in an odd way, I am also very proud." The side project that currently has Kip most proud and involved is a Web site for quadriplegics.

• • •

Laugh When Told Not to Stick Your Head Up

Ann Busby

Work: Helps others discover their own potential

Ann Busby is currently a government employee in training and program management. Some of her most worthwhile work has been as director of child development centers and as an elementary school teacher. Her grandkids are an important part of her life: "My love is my immortality." She is writing to her teenage granddaughter, Britney.

DEAR BRITNEY,

There are things about human nature that will remain constant.

First of all, be true to yourself. I have found this to be my guiding mantra. When times are tough, when tough decisions await, think about how much whatever you decide is going to cost you in time, energy, and ethics. If it's too much, walk away and never look back. Weigh the consequences before making the final choice, but once made, don't waffle.

How do I know this? Oh, let me count the ways! I've found that being true by always keeping my sense of humor not only makes my own life better, but also the lives of the people around me — fellow employees, as well as loved ones.

But sometimes I've failed: One of the jobs I most hoped to get (but didn't) was when the interviewer said she was looking for someone who wanted to have fun at work. What a bizarre concept, right? Have fun at work! In 1986, I went from being known as the "short woman with the big smile" to the grump who was always complaining. Drastic change! I didn't like my environment, and the bosses didn't like me. (To this day I'm convinced it was because they didn't want a woman in management with them. And several women have won EEO suits against them, which shows I'm probably right!) Not only did my peers not like to be around me, but also, your grandfather got tired of hearing me complain. I was always upset.

The day I left that job was the day I started back on the road to being who I wanted to be: The short woman with the big smile.

Afterward, I had the chance to join others in an EEO suit against my former employer. Your grandfather convinced me that if I pursued it, it would just keep me torn up. He was right. I could have won money like the others, but at what cost? So I moved on and am finally happy with myself.

Don't listen to the naysayers of life. They'll say, "The nail that sticks up is the one that gets pounded." But the opposite is true: That nail is the only one to get noticed. When people tell you not to stick your head up, laugh at the thought (never at them). Whether you're just one of the team or the team leader, people follow those who are cheerful and act like they know what they're doing (even if they don't).

I was already pretty good at public speaking (at least I didn't have any fear of being in front of an audience from having been a teacher for seven years) when I became a Toastmaster at age 50. And did I learn many tips for how to keep people's attention! I hope you're never afraid to try new things, even as you grow older and learn more. These days, the more I learn, the more I realize I don't know, after all! Learning is growing. When you quit growing, you quit living. I hope enlightenment, and not fear, will forever be your companion.

Find your strength from within, and share it at every opportunity. In fact, share everything you have and it will return to you in many different ways! I wish nothing but the best for you in your future endeavors, and love you for being you.

You loving grandmother, Ann

Ann Busby reflects, "Most of the passion of youth has bloomed, and my husband and I are now comfortable knowing who we are. Neither of us has ever said, 'Is this all there is?' because family is all that we want."

What Would You Do If You Knew You Could Not Fail?

April Ristau

Work: Shifting from managing projects to managing her life

April Ristau works by day for a large bank as a business analyst, and is a crafty entrepreneur by night — designing and making jewelry. She is writing to Jenna, her 18-year-old cousin, and Conner and Haiden, her 6-year-old and newborn nephews.

DEAR JENNA, CONNER, AND HAIDEN,

This question stares at me every day I'm at my desk.

I'm not really sure when I became afraid of failing. Maybe it was when I started school and was afraid to fail a test. Maybe it was applying to colleges and not getting accepted to all of them. Or maybe it was when I started interviewing for my first "real" job.

I hope that you will never be afraid to fail. I hope that you will always ask yourself: What would I do if I knew I could not fail?

And then do it!

Don't let anything hold you back or let anyone tell you that you can't do something. Most every *can't* is in your head. Most of the time, failure begins with your own beliefs.

I don't want you to be like so many of my friends and family who wish they had done something else with their lives. For some of them, it was because they were afraid of failing. For others, doing what they wanted would take energy and effort and they took the easy route. And yet for others, they were given some roadblocks, so they gave up their dreams. Or maybe, like me, they put those dreams on hold and haven't found the time (or the strength) to go back and put them into action.

My goal for most of my life was to be president of a company, and make a lot of money. So off I went to college, got my degree and planned to be employed making at least $100,000 my first year....After all, I had gone to college! Well, in my first real job I made less than $10,000 (yes, that's four zeros, not five). I quickly learned that my dream of being president of a company was going to take time.

That was almost 20 years ago, and a few times I did lose sight of my goal — but it was always there, in the back of my mind. I am slowly making my way back to that goal, but it has changed slightly. Instead of being president of a large corporation, I am currently the president of my own small company. I hope to do this full-time one day, but for now I am settling on taking baby steps to get there. I know this business may fail, but at least I will have attempted it, and I know that *I* didn't fail. And that is so much better than not ever trying.

So, what will you do since you cannot fail?

April Ristau loves a challenge. That's why she hasn't yet given up on being president of the bank where she works! And why she's completed three marathons and coached hundreds of other people in marathon-running.

Be True to Who You Were Created to Be

Allen Puy

Work: Helps to envision, define, and pursue long-term business possibilities

Allen Puy is a Business Development Enterprise Architect for Lockheed Martin, and is their liaison to technology advances made through Penn State School of Information Sciences and Technology. He is writing to his daughter, four-year-old Grace.

DEAREST GRACE,

One of the toughest things I regularly face is saying goodbye to you when I'll be gone for some time — all day, past your bedtime, or for a few days.

Often, it's work that's taking me away from you. It may be the work I do for Lockheed Martin, the work I do for our church, or the work I do for community theaters — all are a part of my work life. And all hold a place in my heart, but always a smaller part than you and Mommy.

I want you to know what's behind many of my decisions, particularly the ones that take me away from you. It's got a lot to do with my belief about how work needs to fit with life. I've crossed paths with many folks who have trouble reconciling the two. (Sometimes, I'm one of them....) They seem to savor the challenge of finding a work/life balance, of setting aside enough time from work for their life, of finding the right benefits package or vacation schedule or hobbies or volunteer activities to make the formula just right. I've seen my employer and others push work/life programs that they believe will make employees happy, healthy, productive, and loyal.

But I think I've got a different view of making work work. I truly believe that every one of us possesses a particular set of talents — gifts really — that suit us to a particular set of tasks. We find joy and success, by our own inward measures, when we can apply these gifts to serve a larger good.

There *have* been times when work was a four-letter word for me. When I didn't feel that my talents and gifts were being put to use in a valuable way. It may have been a project where I felt my responsibilities were taking me away from my gifts. Or a committee at church I said "yes" to, but should have avoided because my value to the effort was limited. Or overcommitting to a show at the local theater that wasn't using my gifts fairly.

One of those four-letter moments was my first job at my company. I was constantly stressed. I would have dreams about assignments, and would wake up to puzzle over the problems. Yet the stressing and puzzling really didn't help my work or my attitudes. At one point, I just decided not to stress over it anymore. I can't tell you how I was able to just shut it off that way, but it probably had a lot to do with faith and prayer. I had found a key aspect for making my work more satisfying. I really didn't need to be anxious about succeeding or winning new positions; I needed to focus on leveraging the gifts I have, in assignments that can truly benefit from them.

My work included helping employees learn new skills, develop their capabilities, and experience new roles. What fueled me was shepherding them, and acting as a careful steward of a chunk of their lives — a contribution to a larger good. Unfortunately, policies changed, tasks piled on, and I found that I was focused on the drudgery and administrative trivia of management life. I held on as long as I could stand it, but my attitude and drive really started to wane. And I think the team knew it.

That's when I looked to change roles at my company — just like I'd encourage you to do if you ever find yourself in a similar situation.

I've done the same thing at church. (It took me a while to believe that it's not sinful to say "no" to a request from a church committee or leader, reserving my time and energy for larger goods.) For some time, I believed that my gifts for acting and directing would be of most benefit to the congregation if I focused on arranging dramas within the worship services. Yet trusted friends, who knew I had even greater gifts and passions, encouraged me to help lead the actual services. Now, a few years into that role, I've been told that the congregation has truly benefited. I do make poor judgment calls now and then, but since God's in charge, it seems to come out right most of the time.

I find real enjoyment in my work, inside and outside my office. The folks I see who are most unhappy complain of not feeling like they're adding value, that their talents are being put to use, and that what they do really matters. So they find no real joy in what they do.

If you ever find yourself in a place and time where you don't believe all of these are coming together for you, it's time to look for the next place.

I'm not talking about being a quitter. This is about being true to who you were created to be. You were created with gifts to use, to develop, and to enjoy. And as you use them in ways that benefit something more than yourself, they'll grow, and you'll find the joy you deserve.

That should be what work is about — work at home, work at a business, work in ministry, work in the community. And that's how to make sure that work isn't a four-letter word.

Please know that I'll love you always, and I'll always be your daddy.

With all my love,
Daddy

Allen Puy's favorite memories of Grace so far are of her infant days — singing to her as he rocked her to sleep. Allen is involved in music and drama activities in community theater, and at his church. He and his wife and daughter reside in Chester County, Pennsylvania, where he's lived for more than 30 years.

What Is
Your Life's Work?

Field Guide
for Getting Started

Mapping Your Journey

Your extraordinary experience has begun. Among the many gifts these work diaries hold, I would urge you to consider and pay special attention to three....

You graciously accepted the first one, **the Gift of Reflection,** the moment you lingered on a particular passage. During that brief pause, you invited those words in, to amplify the heartbeat of your choices, to dance with your memories, and to shake free all your passions.

My goal in writing *What Is Your Life's Work?* was simple: To stop you, for just a moment, by creating a space for you to think deeply. We're all constantly rushing around, bouncing between the Tyranny of the Urgent and the Opium of Doing Something. It's so rare that we take the time to dwell in silence and thought until greater truths emerge.

Sixty-four work diarists (and a couple thousand just like them) gave you that gift of reflection. They generously shared what usually stays private. In their journal entries and letters are the raw truths and mistakes and discoveries we've all experienced. In their struggles, we see our own. In their letters, we see ourselves. Their main message: *You are not alone.* They've been where you are, and where you are going.

Thank you for pausing long enough to appreciate their gift.

On to the **next steps:** What follows are no-nonsense exercises and checklists for you to capitalize on the Gift of Reflection, as well as **the Gift of Clarity** (tightly articulating what matters to you), and **the Gift of Sharing** (passing your life's work on to others). But first…

Throat-clearing disclaimer: As one letter-writer put it: Honey, there are no shortcuts. Your life's work is *your work.* Nobody hands you answers that are best for you. Certainly not me. If you want something more from this book than reflection, you need to be an active participant. Here are some suggestions for getting started. Select only one, a few, or all of them. It's up to you.

● ● ●

Cherish the Gift of Reflection

Warning: Eight out of every ten readers of this book will do absolutely nothing with it. They'll be all pumped-up while flipping pages, then do nothing that could have changed or enhanced their life's work.

How do I know this? (Besides the fact that most of us avoid any kind of deep reflection.) Because, during the first four years of collecting work diaries, I experienced an 80% drop-off rate from people who made firm commitments to think more deeply about what matters to them. Many who had passionately declared, "I must do this for my son and daughter — it's that important!" soon reneged. "I REALLY wanted to do it," said one. "But I just can't. It's too emotional. I have achieved so little of what I set out to do. I just can't." From another: "I know I said I'd do this for my teenagers, but I am just so swamped. Maybe after my company's latest merger quiets down...."

Ironically, those who most needed to reflect on what matters gave in to the momentary pressures of *morebetterfaster* from bosses, teammates, and customers. Please be among the two out of every ten who do something!

1. Hot-Penning: Record Your Thoughts and Feelings

Hot-penning refers to scribbling your thoughts without ever lifting your pen from the paper (or fingers from the keyboard). Don't stop to ponder, just dump. Record the thoughts and feelings that occurred while you read this book — without judgment or refinement. Did you think or feel anything about:

- How much (or little) you have accomplished?
- What's the price you're willing to pay for what matters?
- What risks should you have taken that you didn't?
- What deserves your precious 1440 minutes every day?
- What doesn't?
- What have you accomplished and not yet celebrated?
- What loss or life-event would force a shift in your life's work?
- What is the legacy of your choices?
- What is the most important thing missing from your life right now?
- What is the most consistent message you've been hearing in your head for the past year?

Goal: To capture your Aha's, Oh-oh's, and Wow's that should not be lost or forgotten

2. Dueling Columns

Separate your daily to-do's into a two-column list:

- **Urgent and Pressured**
- **Important to Me**

The more detailed this list is, the better. (It's OK to have one to-do in both columns.) Then ask yourself three questions:
- Am I happy with what's in each column?
  (Why or why not?)
- How often do I choose to focus on one column over the other?
- Is it time to choose differently?

Goal: To understand how many of your everyday choices and assumptions can be changed, and are within your control

3. Start a Journal

Get yourself a five-dollar-or-under notebook, or set up a blog, or a Word file. Title it something like…
- What Really Matters to Me
- What Is My Life's Work?
- Choices I Made Today
- What I Care About and Believe In

…and just scribble. Do a brain-dump. The key is telling the bare-assed truth, and doing so regularly. (Daily, weekly, or monthly — set a schedule that works for you, and stick to it.)

Goal: To capture your thoughts and feelings, after deep reflection

• • •

Give Yourself the Gift of Clarity

1. Pick Three to Five Letters

Select the letters in this book that speak most directly to you, that grab you, inspire you, teach you, and challenge you.

2. Narrow Your Focus, Find Your Life's Work Theme

You have an advantage that most of the letter-writers in this book did not. It was only after I had read a couple thousand letters that the five discoveries emerged:

- Finding Yourself
- Finding the Lessons to Be Learned, the Questions to Be Asked
- Finding the Choices That Really Matter
- Finding the Courage to Choose
- Finding Joy, Serenity, and Fulfillment

These discoveries are not bound by age or career experience. As you've seen in this book, some teenagers are capable of experiencing the "final" discovery — finding fulfillment — while some retirees still struggle with the "first" — finding themselves. Yet all of us experience all of these discoveries at some point in our journey of figuring out what truly matters.

Odds are that the majority of the letters you selected in Step 1 will fall under one of the five discoveries. Use that as your starting point for your letter. For example:

- If **Finding Yourself** is your theme: Focus on how often you allow daily "fire-fighting" to take you away from what you know is more important. Or focus on the challenge of facing your own fears, or the difficulty of creating quiet time to get to know yourself.
- If **Finding the Courage to Choose** is your theme: Focus on a moment when you made a very difficult choice based on your inner voice, and how difficult that was. Or focus on a moment when you wish you had listened to your inner voice, but didn't.

For additional ideas, see the introduction at the beginning of each discovery. (If your selected letters don't cluster around a particular discovery, just pick any one. You can't go wrong!) Also, check out www.ourlifeswork.com.

Goal: To narrow your focus on what really matters to you, and decide how to use those priorities to make everyday choices

3. Begin a Letter to a Loved One

Select someone who is close to you — son, daughter, dearest friend, closest colleague — and write a letter to him or her about your chosen discovery. Here are some guidelines that letter-writers found extremely helpful:

- While your letter should help those you care about *live the lives* they deserve, it does so by sharing the most important lessons you've learned about *work*. This is important because you then have to **describe how you wrestle with tough work/life choices.**
- **Be truthful.** No spin allowed. Be honest about your accountabilities in all situations.
- **Be yourself.** Write your letter as if you are having a conversation at the kitchen table. Be real!
- **Be specific.** Those who deal with the specifics of good/bad bosses, project deadlines, team dynamics, etc., reveal more of their thinking that others would find valuable. Those who stay at the *Be True to Yourself* 30,000-foot-high level rarely reveal anything helpful.
- **Tell stories.** One way to push past *Be True to Yourself* platitudes is to tell stories about how you lived (or did not live) what truly matters.
- **Be vulnerable**. Powerful letters and journal entries expose our frailties and our mistakes, and share the really tough lessons. If your letter is not hard to write — or not a little embarrassing, a little too revealing — it probably has not gone far enough.

Goal: To begin to articulate your life's work — how you continually figure out what matters and what doesn't — with greater clarity, honesty, and depth than you ever have before.

What I've witnessed: People who felt they were *consistently* focused on what really matters had experienced three or more of the five discoveries, and could clearly articulate the *how*, *when*, and *why* of each of those experiences. Clarity is the key!

4. Continue Your Journey at www.ourlifeswork.com
- Additional downloadable letters and excerpts
- Workshops, presentations
- Additional how-to tools and support for letter-writing
- Community space for sharing stories and experiences
- **Bonus:** Get YOUR letter in the paperback version!
  We are taking submissions for additional letters.
  We will select the most powerful letter(s) for inclusion
  in the paperback version of *What Is Your Life's Work?*

• • •

Share the Gift of Clarity With Your Loved Ones

Helen Harvey (page 22) approached me and said, "We're having a lot of difficulty dealing with John getting fired. I know John is writing a letter about that [page 20], would you mind if I asked our kids to write letters to him too?" Mind? Heck, no!

The Harvey family embodies the ultimate outcome from these letters. They not only wrote down what really mattered, their letters jumpstarted completely new discussions, and became the foundation for new and different family decisions.

It's almost impossible to stop these new conversations!

From Don Blohowiak, a leadership coach: "I simply handed my letter to my sons, who are both in their twenties. In separate conversations, THEY both raised workplace challenges that segued into life discussions I had been meaning to have with them."

From someone who read the Harveys' letters before deciding to write her own: "My husband is expecting to be one of the next 9,000 to feel the ax at his company. That family's letters have been very cathartic for my daughter and me. We've been able to openly express how we feel, and what we need to do to 'help Dad' and help the family. You cannot imagine the power of these letters."

Here's how to get the conversation started:

1. Share Your Letter With Your Loved Ones

2. Don't Manage the Conversation
Let them come to you with curiosity and questions.

3. Be as Truthful, Specific, and Vulnerable in Your Conversation as You Were in Your Letter
If you are, something extraordinary will happen. You will get back more than you give. Suddenly, you'll experience even greater clarity about rights and wrongs, what matters and what doesn't, how and when to follow your passions.

• • •

The Invitation

During the past year, I have done a lot of reflection and made many changes in my life. On one business trip, I spent an entire day walking the streets of Singapore in 100° heat, dripping sweat onto a tattered journal. One of the questions I pondered was: "What are my dreams?" One of my answers was: "To make a difference for as many people as possible."

I've taken this book as far as I can. It needs you to be complete. I won't have made a difference unless you do something with it.

I close with an excerpt from Oriah Mountain Dreamer's prose pose, *The Invitation*:

It doesn't interest me what you do for a living.
I want to know what you ache for, and if you dare to
dream of meeting your heart's longing.
It doesn't interest me how old you are.
I want to know if you will risk looking like a fool for love,
for your dream, for the adventure of being alive....

...I want to know if you can be alone with yourself
and if you truly like the company you keep
in the empty moments.

Acknowledgments

Thanks!

These are the people who made sure I was focused on what matters:

Family. Thank you, Louise and Ian, for all your support, love, and laughter through all the years and all the crazy projects like this one. That last hug in our kitchen will last me a lifetime. Ian, you are the best thing that ever happened to me. Ever! Mom, I'm trying to remember all you taught me. Hopefully, I'm doing OK on following my passions, dreams, creativity, and values.

● ● ●

Donna, thank you so much for entering my life. You showed me new paths to joy. For that, I am eternally grateful.

● ● ●

And these are the people who made sure I stayed true to you:

Book Teammates. I owe Herb Schaffner, Marion Maneker, Keith Pfeffer, and Steve Hanselman at HarperCollins soooooo much. They saw the potential in this project and provided amazing support in shaping this book. Especially Herb, who guided me every step of the way, held my hand, provided air cover, and made sense of my words on a daily basis....Thank you all for everything!

Before Herb saw anything, my agents Howard Yoon (who is becoming a first-time dad as I write this!) and Gail Ross shaped my rough idea (originally titled *Work Diaries*) into something the market would buy, and then found a home for it at HarperCollins. And before them was Lisa Adams. Without your original support, Lisa, none of this would have happened. To each of you: You're the best!

Design and Production. With two kids crawling or crying nearby, and with the patience of a saint, my production buddy, Aimee Leary at Final Art, transformed my scribbles into wonderful page designs. Mark and Matt Versaggi worked tirelessly on the e-companion site, www.ourlifeswork.com. Leah Carlson-Stanisic and Donna Ruvituso oversaw pre-press production and printing, Mucca Design created the wonderful cover that grabbed your attention, Sharon Johnson indexed the book, and Adelle Krauser dotted every "i" in the copyediting and proofing process. These are the talented people who turned my words into something useful, helpful, and eye-catching. I'm extremely grateful to each of you. Thanks!

• • •

And these are the people who gave you a voice in this book:

Work Diarists. I didn't really author this book. You did, or people who are just like you. Thousands of people who were either searching in the dark for something different, or who had flashlights, pointing the way. This is their book, their story, and your book, your story. My job was to provide a safe and inviting space for people to share their innermost fears, concerns, passions, and thoughts. And then to share with you what I have learned. I hope I have been a good guardian of your shared story.

• • •

My inspiration. You! Thank you. I look forward to seeing you on my bike trip around the world, hitting every brewery I can find.

Endnotes & Stats

The Five Most Important Things I've Learned

Since 1992 I have been researching how we get stuff done. I refer you to www.simplerwork.com for white papers and free downloadable tools designed to make your day easier and clearer. Here I'd like to share why that research has caused me to be such an outspoken gadfly against the corporate stupidity that wastes your time, attention, and dreams.

• • •

1. The Number One Behavior in Business Today Is Moving To Do's onto Someone Else's Plate.

Most everyone is under-resourced, with too little time and too many to-do's. So they respond to new to-do's the only way they can: Triage (doing just enough to keep things moving) whatever can't be passed on to others, and then move the remaining to-do's on to as many teammates and subordinates as possible.

The Big So What: You should be questioning a lot more of what you are asked to do. Many of those requests are other people's priorities, not yours.

• • •

2. Three of the Five Biggest Timewasters in Your Day Are Communication-Based.

For most knowledge and service workers, (1) unfocused and unnecessary meetings, (2) cluttered incoming communication, and (3) responding to all requests for communication waste a minimum of two hours every day! For some, up to four hours! **The Big So What:** What *doesn't* matter is all the clutter and crap that comes at you from well-meaning (but triaging) teammates and managers. Delete, delete, delete…focus, focus, focus!

• • •

3. Staying Focused Is an Act of Courage.

I have asked people around the world to rank-order work-related activities on a scale of 1 to 10, with 1 being "No sweat; no courage at all" and 10 being "Cold sweat; I could never do that!" Deleting emails, saying "no" to a boss or colleague, and skipping meetings that are known to be a waste of time routinely rank 6.5 to 7 on the courage meter — equal to actions such as whistle-blowing or facing a difficult ethical dilemma. What's wrong with this picture?

The Big So What: Diarist Linda Stone said it best: Attention is your scarcest resource. Be courageous in how you spend your attention and you will be repaid with balance, fulfillment, achievement, and energy. Be fearful of missing an email or a call, or of saying "no" to all the requests for your attention, and you will be repaid with less and less control over your future.

• • •

4. 1440 Drives a Lot More Behavior Than We Realize.

(1440 being the number of minutes in a day.) Leaders and managers think of hierarchy, strategies, culture, loyalty, rewards, and recognition when they wish to drive human behavior. Yet my research has shown that making work tools and information easier to use, and designing workflows and communication to save people time, often get faster, better, and cheaper results!

The Big So What: Leaders and managers must make *Ease of Use* and *Reduced Use of Time* top priorities. Those who do so will be rewarded with easier, better paths to success. Those who don't are being disrespectful of their teammates by wasting too much of their precious 1440 minutes.

• • •

5. You Are Free to Choose.

No matter where I go in the world I constantly hear: "But you don't understand, my boss (or culture, or customer, or the competition) won't let me choose differently. Even though I know I'm not doing what matters, I *have* to do it this way." **The Big So What:** No, you don't. God put you on this planet to choose. Make sure your choices are your own. Not someone else's!

Quick-Search Index

Finding the Themes That Matter to You

While I found five main discoveries across all of these intimate exchanges, your daily challenges rarely present themselves in such tidy packages. Real work and real-life situations are often messy, jumbled, and foggy.

That's why I searched for common themes that cut across all the discoveries. I found a dozen such themes spread throughout the letters and journal entries:

- Adversity or Trauma
- Appreciation and Blessings
- Faith, Spirituality, Service
- Family, Relationships, and Love
- Inner Voice, Dreams, Fulfillment, Joy
- Intolerable Situations, Displacement
- Learning, Growth
- Opportunities, Choices, Do the Right Thing
- Priorities, Focus
- Rebellion, Risk, Fear
- Truth, Leadership, Courage
- Work Ethic, Discipline

On the following pages I've designed a table for you to quickly search which diarists addressed which themes. Of course, you'll find many sub-themes as you dig into each letter. (For example, *Stay-at-Home Parenting* occurs often as a sub-theme under *Family*.) But to speed your search, I tried to keep the table focused on the three-to-five core themes that each letter-writer expressed.

Jump in and jump around! The power of the diarists' words remain intact in any order you choose to read them.

Discovery	Person	Page	Adversity or Trauma	Appreciation and Blessings	Faith, Spirituality, Service
1	Lisa Hesmondhalgh	17			
	John Harvey	20			
	Helen Harvey	22	●		
	Janean Harvey Corinne Harvey John Harvey, Jr.	24	●	●	
	Jacquelyn Rardin	28	●		
	Ariel Blair	33	●		
	Paul Buckley	36			
	Anonymous	37	●		
	Marshall Goldsmith	38			
	Jody Lentz	40			
	Mary Zisk	41			
	Tami Belt	44			
	Jane Puckett	45			
	Dennis Bonilla	48	●		
	Nancy Adler	52			
2	Linda Stone	61			
	Sue Brooks	65			
	Neal Sofian	66			●